From my personal experience, I know the power of prophecy in charting the course of a believer's life. Pastor Femi's new book sheds much light on this all-important subject. His personal experiences that he shares in the book will encourage and inspire anyone who desires to fulfil their prophetic purpose in life.

Israel Emmanuel, *Author, The Shift of A Lifetime*

Prophecy is simply knowing the mind of God in the past so we can decipher the present and take a leap into the future. The Word of God is a great book on prophecy where we can know what to believe God for in life. This masterpiece has simplified the subject of prophecy and made it accessible to all who desire to operate in their *kairos* moments. Welcome to the future as you take your place in God's prophetic agenda for the earth today and take the lead in your sphere of influence.

Ayo Daniels, *Pastor, The Lighthouse, Nigeria*

Prophecy is one of the most misunderstood and erroneously taught subjects of our time. It is essential that this generation of believers are properly equipped and trained in the study of prophesy and its operations. In *Unlock Your Future!*, Pastor

Femi Adun opens the eyes of his readers to a life of blessing and spiritual success that is available to them through the divine power of prophecy. He powerfully unveils Scripture upon Scripture to show what prophecy is and is not. Readers will walk away with clarity and understanding of the will of God concerning their lives.

Pastor Femi Adun carries an anointing for revelation and teaching the Word of God. The book you are holding is an out-pour of that anointing. May the eyes of your understanding be enlightened as you read this prophetic guide to *Unlock Your Future!*

Evangelist Azizah Morrison,

AzizahSpeaks Ministries & Enterprises USA

Prophecies don't fulfil themselves. It is expedient that individuals, families, churches, organisations and entire nations become ultimately responsible to their prophecy per time. In very practical ways Pastor Femi Adun expounds on how you can take delivery of your prophecy in God. His life and ministry has been punctuated by prophecy and powered by grace. Indeed, this is not a story book but a prophetic manual to glory.

Gideon Mba, *Author, Sent*

Femi Adun, a man totally dedicated to the kingdom, passionate, zealous and full of the Spirit, has put together life-changing truths on the topic of prophecy. The book is a great read and full of insight that includes every believer as a beneficiary and possible participant in the prophetic. This is rare, very useful and highly commendable. I pray the book goes out to inspire believers all over the world and challenge them to embrace an invaluable weapon in God's arsenal: *Prophecy!*

Rev. Lekan Fasina, *Pastor, Ignite Church, UK*

UNLOCK YOUR FUTURE!

HOW PROPHECY CAN GUIDE YOU TO YOUR DESTINY

UNLOCK YOUR FUTURE!

HOW PROPHECY CAN GUIDE YOU TO YOUR DESTINY

FEMI ADUN

SOPHOS
SB
BOOKS

Raising the voice of wisdom!

Unlock Your Future!

Copyright © 2012 by Femi Adun

Published by

SOPHOS Books

15 North Downs Road

Croydon

CR0 0LE

SOPHOS Books is an Emmanuel Publishing imprint

ISBN 978-1-905669-01-1

All Scripture quotations are taken from the *New King James* version of the Bible.
Used by permission.
Scriptures marked AMP are from the Amplified Bible.
Scriptures marked The Message are from The Message Bible.

Cover design by *Maestro Creativity*

Book preparation by *emmanuelpublishing.com*

Printed in the EU

Contents

To three people who have served as prophets over my life
through their love, words and action:

My mum, Mrs. Adebisi Adun,
who first saw who I am in Christ and
loved me in spite of all negatives.

My Prophet, Pastor Sam Adeyemi,
who on several occasions continue to
remind me of who I am in Christ through
his prophetic declarations as well as wise counsels.

My lover, Busola Adun,
who believed what my mother saw,
believed my pastors' convictions about my destiny
and acted on it by saying "yes I do"

Acknowledgements

Every new book is truly like another child! They are a work of love. They are conceived in intimacy with the Lord Himself, prayed over by hundreds, watched by many, coached by a few, and then there is that actual labour.

Sincerely speaking, *Unlock Your Future!* had to pass through these stages to be in your hands right now. Therefore, it will be a great injustice to act like it was all my individual effort.

I continue to thank God for the rock from which I am hewed. My tutelage under the spiritual parenthood of Pastor Sam & Nike Adeyemi has been a rock solid foundation for my continuous growth and success in life & ministry. Busola & I are eternally grateful to you both!

Special thanks To Dr. Hugh Osgood, a gift from God to me and to whom I now receive as my apostolic covering.

That you could take time to write the introduction for this book blessed me, but going the extra mile to actually edit the script really touched. Your words and deeds truly teach me the mark of a true Apostle.

Pastor Dayo Fasina, thanks for proof reading this book. What a great job you did.

God knew I had to meet you, Pastor Israel Emmanuel, when we preached together at the same conference in Nigeria. It is difficult to express in words how much of a blessing you are to me. I thank God I obeyed Him when He instructed me to submit my script to you. THANK YOU!

Pastor Gideon Mba, you are truly a kingdom general! I am forever grateful for the covenant relationship we share and your commitment to the fulfilment of my destiny.

To the entire family of *Grace House International Ministry*, thank you for allowing me first share some of the principles in this book with you as well as your genuine submission to God's calling upon my life. I love being your pastor everyday!

To my beloved siblings, Osa Adun, Oladunni Okpame, Isoken Nwagor & Morenike Adun. I appreciate your constant love & support over these years. God bless you all!

I also appreciate the numerous ministries I had the privileged of sharing some of the insights in this book. Thank you pastors, I will never take your pulpit for granted.

Special thanks to Pastor Ayo Daniels and Pastor Seyi Oladimeji for your longstanding and genuine believe in me. May the Lord honour you both.

Pastor Seun Ladokun, Pastor Oluwagbenga Ajibola & Pastor Leke Idowu. True sons of the prophet! I salute the fearful courage you guys possess.

Big thanks to everyone whose name I could not mention due to time and space. God bless you all.

Finally, to my generals Joella and Israel Adun, you both are signs that God's word over my life is SURE. Thanks for teaching me how to enjoy my life!

Foreword

Prophecy is central to the Christian experience. Prophecy is simply divinely inspired utterance and it is ordained by God to give us encouragement and direction. Hebrews 11:3 says; *"Through faith we understand that the worlds were framed by the word of God, so that the things which are seen were not made from things which are visible."*

This implies that prophecy literarily shapes our world. And to guarantee that we will never be in short supply of heaven's resources for shaping our world, Joel prophesied, *"And it shall come to pass afterward, that I will pour out my Spirit on all flesh; your sons and your daughters shall prophesy..."* (Joel 2:28). Paul the Apostle also admonishes us to *"pursue love, and desire spiritual gifts, but especially that you may prophesy"* (1 Corinthians 14:1).

We cannot fully realise our potentials until we are tuned in to God's frequency. *"But there is a spirit in man, and the* breadth of the Almighty gives him understanding" (Job 32:8). When we on God's frequency, we get revelation. We gain insight. We get direction. We experience spiritual growth. Although some have had their (spiritual) fingers burnt seeking direction through prophecies because it is subject to a lot of abuse, the bible encourages us not to despise prophesying (1Thessalonians 5:20).

In *Unlock Your Future!*, Femi Adun, with Scriptures and personal experience, shares basic principles that will help us to identify genuine prophecy and to effectively apply it to our lives. He passionately expresses his desire to see people experience the supernatural through every sentence in this book.

Although prophecy is a subject that some try to mystify and which could be expressed with complexity, he has tried to keep it simple enough for us to understand and apply to our lives. I pray that everyone who reads this book will experience a deeper walk with the Holy Spirit, and a new dimension of God's wisdom and power.

Sam Adeyemi
Daystar Christian Centre, Lagos, Nigeria.

Introduction

Femi Adun has provided us with a helpful book at a time when many around the world are focusing on personal prophecy as a key to discerning God's will.

Over many years in ministry I have benefitted from the wise counsel of friends. When I was a young man I was particularly grateful for the mentoring I received from those who sought the Lord so they could help and guide me. Such counsel proved invaluable, coming as it did alongside my personal relationship with God, built up through Bible reading and prayer.

One of the highlights of this book is the way that Pastor Femi seeks to give practical advice on how to relate to those who mentor us. He does this having taken us through a step-by-step guide to understanding personal prophecy: its nature, limits and strengths; the principles for accessing and activating prophetic words; the hindrances and helps to watch for along the way; and a concluding emphasis on the pre-eminence of God's grace.

At a time when different Christian traditions have divergent ways of viewing the role of personal prophecy, this book sets out some helpful principles. Pastor Femi's willingness to share from personal experience, as well as to engage with Scripture, keeps the book truly practical.

There are valuable lessons and some sensible safeguards here for those seeking personal guidance. Femi's transparency also means that there are insights here for those wanting to weigh the priority that many internationally are currently giving to personal prophetic input.

My prayer is that you will be open to receive all that the Lord has for you as you discover your destiny in Him – through your personal relationship with the Almighty, your grasp of His written word and through the wise prophetic counsel of those who faithfully seek God on your behalf.

Thank you, Femi, for all that you have shared with us.

Dr. Hugh Osgood,

President, CiC International

Author's Preface

The subject of prophecy has been mystified to the extent that many Christians can no longer relate with it as God intended. It is critical for everyone born of God to have an adequate understanding of prophecy in its most simple and practical form.

In the Bible, the word *prophecy* is sometimes used generally for different kinds of divine utterances. It is also used specifically to refer to a gift and manifestation of the Holy Spirit. This distinction is important for comprehending prophecy in its widest scope.

Prophecy, when activated, is a live wire that brings us into the fullness of God's plans and purposes for our lives. Without it, we may live our entire lives based on assumption, which is said to be the lowest level of knowledge. Prophecy is one of God's tools for bringing an individual, a group of people or an entire nation into His predestined plan.

Naturally, we came into the world ignorant of our destiny. No baby was born with the knowledge of what he was going to become. The knowledge is revealed over time as the child grows up. This is also true of nations. I once heard my mentor say, *"You are not born to determine your purpose or assignment, you are born to discover it"*. God has made it easy for us to discover what we were created to do, either through His written word – the Bible - or spoken word - through the operation of prophecy.

Throughout the Bible, God demonstrated the importance of prophecy. He showed how He used it to bring His children into their prepared blessings and how He has used it to deliver nations from their enemies. Everyone has a prophecy over his/her life whether he/she knows it. Whether you like it or not, it is there! But it is not just our knowledge of it that counts but an understanding of its role in our lives and how we can connect with it.

Friend, this book is not a story book and should not be read as one. It is rather a guide to unlocking your glorious destiny through the ministry of the prophetic.

Let the journey of truth begin!

1

*What
Is
Prophecy?*

The easiest way to know what something is *not* is to know what it is. Likewise to know what a false prophecy is, we need to know what a genuine one is. I have come across a lot of people who have accepted what God does not have in His agenda for them just because a prophet said it. The greatest harm you can do to yourself is to believe in the wrong thing.

In this chapter, I want to share with you what I have come to learn about prophecy in my years of walking with the Lord. I encourage you to read carefully, meditate on and grasp the thoughts before you move on to the next chapter.

1. Prophecy is God's word declared in the present, backed by His Spirit to assure and create His desired future concerning a person, people or nation.

What this means is that before a word declared over a person, group of people or a nation can be accepted as a genuine prophetic word, it must agree and align with what the Scriptures say. It must be declared in a Holy Spirit-filled atmosphere or by someone who is genuinely filled with the Spirit of God and it can be futuristic.

> "Then Elisha said, "Hear the word of the LORD. Thus says the LORD: Tomorrow about this time a seah (measure) of fine flour shall be sold for a shekel, and two seahs (measure) of barley for a shekel, at the gate of Samaria."
>
> **(2 Kings 7:1)**

Prophecies reveal God's future plan for His people or a nation. Prophecies don't reveal events of the past or the present. As we noticed in the above scripture, the prophet Elisha revealed God's plan to the king of Israel. These words were not analyzing the difficult times the king and his people were going through, and how terrible their situation had become. Elisha's prophecy revealed a way out. A futuristic revelation is one of the elements of a prophetic word.

Also, in John 6:63 Jesus Christ said, "*It is the Spirit who gives life; the flesh profits nothing. The words that I speak to you are spirit and they are life.*"

Prophecy is not the words of a man (even though God uses men and women to reveal His counsel). This is why it is dangerous to build one's life on what a man says and not what God says. I place emphasis on the fact that *prophecies must be backed by the Spirit of God.*

Firstly, it is the Spirit that gives men insight into the agenda of God for people or nations.

> "But there is [a vital force] a spirit [of intelligence] in man, and the breath of the Almighty gives men understanding"

Here we learn that the Spirit of God is also the spirit of intelligence. Word Web dictionary defines *intelligence* as 'the ability to comprehend; to understand and profit from experience'. Without the ability to comprehend what God's plans for your life are, it will be difficult for you to take advantage of them and have the ability to profit from each experience you encounter along the way in your journey of life. To have the Spirit of intelligence also means to understand why you are here on earth and what God intends for you. Many have been blown away by wrong doctrines because they lack the understanding of how God operates uniquely in every individual. The Bible says "for *it is God that works in you both to will and to do for His good pleasure*" (Philippians 2:13). This makes it very crucial to operate by the Spirit of intelligence in order to know exactly what God's will for your life is and what He wants you to do to achieve it.

Secondly, the actualizing power comes also from the Holy Spirit.

"Seek out of the book of the Lord and read: not
one of these [details of prophecy] shall fail, none
shall want and lack her mate [in fulfilment]. For
the mouth [of the Lord] has commanded, and
His Spirit has gathered them."

(Isaiah 34:16 AMP)

In the above scripture, the word of the Lord says it is the
Holy Spirit that has the responsibility of actualizing God's
promise in our lives. In Acts 1:8, hear what Jesus Christ said
to His disciples in order to fulfil what had been spoken
concerning them.

"But you shall receive power when the Holy
Spirit has come upon you; and you shall be wit-
nesses to Me in Jerusalem, and in all Judea and
Samaria, and to the ends of the earth."

(Acts 1:8)

Without the involvement of the Holy Spirit, God's
prophecy over your life will be held bound. It has to be
overshadowed by the Holy Spirit. This is why it is very
important to submit your life to declarations backed by the
Spirit of God.

In the book of 1 Samuel chapter 10, the Bible records that
when the Spirit of God came upon Saul, he began to
prophesy with other prophets. Saul wasn't a prophet because
in that same passage of the scripture, the people around who

heard Saul prophesy were surprised that he did. The Holy Spirit is the revealer of the secret things that belong to God. Saul was only a vessel amplifying the voice of the true speaker who is God, made possible by His Spirit.

> "When they came there to the hill, there was a group of prophets to meet him; then the Spirit of God came upon him, and he prophesied among them. And it happened, when all who knew him formerly saw that he indeed prophesied among the prophets, that the people said to one another, "What is this that has come upon the son of Kish? Is Saul also among the prophets?" Then a man from there answered and said, "But who is their father?" Therefore it became a proverb: "Is Saul also among the prophets?" And when he had finished prophesying, he went to the high place."
>
> **(I Samuel 10:10-13)**

There is a scripture that accentuates this in detail. It is 1 Corinthians 2:6-16:

> "However, we speak wisdom among those who are mature, yet not the wisdom of this age, nor of the rulers of this age, who are coming to nothing. But we speak the wisdom of God in a mystery, the hidden wisdom which God ordained before the ages for our glory, which none of the rulers of this age knew; for had they known, they would not have crucified the Lord

of glory. But as it is written;

"Eye has not seen, nor ear heard, nor have entered into the heart of man the things which God has prepared for those who love Him." But God has revealed them to us through His Spirit. For the Spirit searches all things, yes, the deep things of God. For what man knows the things of a man except the spirit of the man which is in him? Even so no one knows the things of God except the Spirit of God.

Now we have received, not the spirit of the world, but the Spirit who is from God, that we might know the things that have been freely given to us by God. These things we also speak, not in words which man's wisdom teaches but which the Holy Spirit teaches, comparing spiritual things with spiritual. But the natural man does not receive the things of the Spirit of God, for they are foolishness to him; nor can he know them, because they are spiritually discerned. But he who is spiritual judges all things, yet he himself is rightly judged by no one. For "who has known the mind of the LORD that he may instruct Him?" But we have the mind of Christ."

(1 Corinthians 2:6-16)

Paul, the writer of this passage of the Bible, states it clearly here that it is the Spirit that reveals the deep things of God in order to help us know the things that have been freely given to us. He says natural men (those who are not saved through Jesus Christ) cannot receive the things of the Spirit realm. This is why I say it is dangerous to accept declarations over your life when you are not sure of the source. Some men and women go around calling themselves prophets and prophetesses, prophesying what they have not heard from God. The sad news is that many Christians fall into their trap (see Ezekiel 13). The only reason this kind of evil happens to a believer is because s/he has neglected her/his devotion with God. Jesus said "My sheep hear my voice", meaning that we can recognize the voice of God or the word of God declared by a prophet.

Recently, I had the opportunity to encourage a young lady over the internet. She asked me to pray for her to experience God's blessings, favour and patience. So I told her that the most important point amongst her three prayer requests is patience. She asked for the reason I said this and I told her that patience for God's prophecy over her life will make it come to pass and all other blessings will follow. Again, she said "I don't understand prophecy" and I explained to her that prophecy is God's spoken word to bless and unlock the treasure in her future and that if there isn't a direct prophecy spoken to her, she can locate any promise in the Bible and make it her prophecy. I did not want her to start looking for a prophecy and then fall into the traps of false prophets. Having a prophecy to run with is this simple: God's word is full prophecy for every believer.

In Ezekiel chapter 13, the word of the Lord came to Ezekiel, a true prophet of God, against false prophets, who had been prophesying lies to God's people:

> "Son of man, prophesy against the prophets of Israel who prophesy, and say to those who prophesy out of their own heart, hear the word of the Lord, thus says the Lord God: "Woe to the foolish prophets, who follow their own spirit and have seen nothing! O Israel, your prophets are like foxes in the deserts. You have not gone up into the gaps to build a wall for the house of Israel to stand in battle on the day of the Lord. They have envisioned futility and false divination, saying, 'Thus says the Lord!' But the Lord has not sent them; yet they hope that the word may be confirmed. Have you not seen a futile vision, and have you not spoken false divination? You say, 'The Lord says,' but I have not spoken." Therefore thus says the Lord God: "Because you have spoken nonsense and envisioned lies, therefore I am indeed against you," says the Lord God."
>
> **(Ezekiel 13:1-8)**

The issue of false prophets and prophecies has been in existence since Ezekiel's days and it is still prevalent today. But once there is a proper knowledge of the subject based on the word of God, then more people and nations will be set free from foxes in the deserts - false prophets. It is really sad that the house of God, the place where God's children ought to enjoy direction via His word, has now become the house of foxes. So many believers, especially the younger ones, have fallen into the traps of false prophets and have been misled by false declarations made over their lives, in the same way as the children of Israel fell for false direction when Moses went up into the mountain to receive the commandments of the Lord. It cost all of them their lives and this was not meant to be. This is what happens to us each time we base our life on false prophecies; we lose something that we might never be able to recover.

Some of the wise kings recorded in the Old Testament knew it wasn't safe going to battle without hearing from God and that was why they sought after prophets. Imagine what would happen if the entire army of a nation follows the direction of a false prophet and went to war with a stronger nation God has not conquered on their behalf? The result would be catastrophic!

2. Prophecy is God's active word spoken to reveal the fulfilment of a later event.

Every word from God is active; it is either doing something or requires the receiver to do something in order to get His purpose fulfilled. In Genesis, when Abraham received a prophetic word from God, it was active in nature - *"I will make you a father of many nations"*. The word 'make' is an active word; prophecy does something or makes something happen. God doesn't say what He is wishing to do in our lives, ministries or nation; He declares what He is doing or will do. This is another attribute of a true Prophecy!

> "So shall My word be that goes forth from My mouth; It shall not return to Me void, But it shall **accomplish** what I please, And it shall prosper in the thing for which I sent it."
>
> **(Isaiah 55:11)**

The word 'accomplish' is defined as 'Cause to happen; complete successfully'. A true prophetic word from God is and will forever be active in nature. Dr. T.L Osborn in his message 'Anointed and appointed' said, "There is energy in God's spoken word to create results of its kind". In the book of Genesis where an account of the creation of heaven and earth is recorded, the Bible states it clearly that it was the spoken word of God that achieved all that God created. The word 'let', which is an action word, was used several times by God to institute the world we live in today.

In Isaiah 9:6, God gave a prophetic word concerning the birth of Jesus Christ and His assignment through Prophet Isaiah,

> **"For unto us a Child is born, unto us a Son is given; and the government will be upon His shoulder. And His name will be called Wonderful, Counselor, Mighty God, Everlasting Father, and Prince of Peace."**
>
> **(Isaiah 9:6)**

Looking carefully at Isaiah's prophecy, the phrase "will be" was mentioned twice, which shows that genuine prophecies from God are always active in effect. God does not say that something 'may be', He says 'will be'. In other words God's declaration over us as individuals or a nation is not based on probability but on certainty. It's active and definite!

My pastor, Sam Adeyemi, always says, "The word works wonders!" That means the word of God doesn't just say what wonders God can perform in your life but can and will perform wonders in your life. One word from God can change your life. On many occasions, Jesus Christ healed people who had been oppressed for years by just saying "go your way and be healed". The word works if you can take it as final authority over your life!

In the name of Jesus, I command every setback in your life, family or ministry to give way for your miracle! Amen.

3. Prophecy is God's plan for us revealed to us through His word in order for us to lay hold on it.

What God wants for us His beloved children is not unreachable. He is not a difficult Father. He would not say to anyone, "Here is what I have planned for you but you can't have it". Every word from God concerning our future is reachable, touchable and achievable! When God revealed to Joseph in a dream that he was going to be greater than his brothers, in spite of the obstacles that confronted and contended with the reality of the prophecy, God's word still came to pass. Joseph did not only become greater than his brothers, God made him very great in Egypt.

Looking back into my journey in life, I have come to realise that no matter what we experience, in adherence to the principles of God's word, His word over our lives will definitely be fulfilled. Even though I was created for something positive and great, I went in the opposite direction of God's prophetic word concerning my destiny for over two decades. There was no way I could relate to becoming anything anyone would want to identify with, much less impacting nations. No way! By the time I turned 20, I had committed nearly every sin the world offered. I was a very wayward boy. But my mother had received a prophetic word concerning my future that I would be a preacher of God's word. Inspired by this word, she kept confessing it, praying and believing it until there was an encounter. I got saved and Jesus Christ got hold of me and changed my life even till this day. Today my books, messages and meetings have blessed countless people all over the world.

What I have learnt is that negative circumstances only come to validate the authenticity of God's word over our lives and not to negate it.

In his album, *New Season,* Israel Houghton said, "Our problems don't equal our prophecies."

No matter how big the challenges may be, they don't stand a chance against what God has said or is saying concerning your future. Apostle Paul understood this so much that in spite of his suffering, he said,

> "…in stripes above measure, in prisons more frequently, in deaths often. From the Jews five times I received forty stripes minus one. Three

times I was beaten with rods; once I was stoned;
three times I was shipwrecked; a night and a day
I have been in the deep; in journeys often, in
perils of waters, in perils of robbers, in perils of
my own countrymen, in perils of the Gentiles, in
perils in the city, in perils in the wilderness, in
perils in the sea, in perils among false brethren;
in weariness and toil, in sleeplessness often, in
hunger and thirst, in fastings often, in cold and
nakedness."

(2 Corinthians 11:23-27)

Yet Paul could still say,

"For I consider that the sufferings of this present
time are not worthy to be compared with the
glory (prophecy) which shall be revealed in us."

(Romans 8:18)

Now my question is, what are you going through that
makes you feel it is over for you? Have you gone through
what Paul went through? It is not a fable. It was real and yet
his eyes were kept on the fulfilment of God's word over his
life. Paul could have said, "Oh! I am just a load of rubbish,"
but he did not think like that. He had an understanding that
his suffering did not negate the prophecy declared by
Ananias in Acts 9:15: *"But the Lord said to him (Ananias), "Go,
for he (Paul) is a chosen vessel of Mine to bear My name before
Gentiles, kings, and the children of Israel."*

Every one of us, like Paul, is chosen to stand before kings and queens. We are created with authority and influence. In Revelation 5:10, God declares that He *"has made us kings and priests to our God; and we shall reign on the earth."* Any situation that puts you under and not on top is not permitted to remain in your life. Every situation of shame bows to you in the precious name of Jesus Christ, Amen!

Prophecies are not declared over you to magnify your mountains or barriers. On the contrary, prophecies will magnify what beauty God can bring out of your life in spite of your past or present ugly situation. The Bible says, *"God calls things that are not (physically) as though they were"* (see Romans 4:17). This means that God's declaration over our situations shows the possibility of a way out of that calamity into a prepared blessing.

Prophecy does not explain the potency of God in a given situation or circumstances; it confirms His supremacy.

2

The Characteristics Of Prophecy

There are two characteristics of prophecy, as found in the Bible, that are necessary for its function and purpose. We will now consider these below.

1. Prophecy is fractional

According to Paul in 1 Corinthians 13:9 he said, *"For we know in part and we prophesy in part".*

An important characteristic of prophecy is that it is fractional. It comes in part. No person has the totality of what God is saying to the Body of Christ. Prophecy is given in part, which makes it progressive revelation. This makes it essential for us to build a devotional relationship with God in order to receive more of His plans for our life. The Amplified version of I Corinthians 13:9 reads;

> "For our knowledge is fragmentary (incomplete and imperfect), and our prophecy (our teaching) is fragmentary (incomplete and imperfect)."
>
> **(I Corinthians 13:9 AMP)**

God's word concerning His plans for us is fragmented and until we receive it in full, it remains incomplete and imperfect. This doesn't make God's word imperfect; it simply means that until His plan for our lives are fully fulfilled, we can't say we have reached the place of God's perfect will for our lives.

> "And do not be conformed to this world, but be transformed by the renewing of your mind, that you may prove what is that good and acceptable and **perfect will** of God."
>
> **(Romans 12:2)**

A good example of this can be found in Genesis 22, when God spoke to Abraham to give up his only son, whom he loved, as a sacrificial offering. Immediately, Abraham embarked on a journey in obedience to God to sacrifice Isaac. On getting to the place where he would slaughter the young lad, God spoke to Abraham again saying;

> "Do not lay your hand on the lad, or do anything to him; for now I know that you fear God, since you have not withheld your son, your only son, from Me. since you have not withheld your son, your only son, from Me." Then Abraham lifted his eyes and looked, and there behind him was a ram caught in a thicket by its horns. So Abraham went and took the ram, and offered it up for a burnt offering instead of his son."
>
> **(Genesis 22:13)**

What would have happened if Abraham did not pay attention to God's further instructions? He would have killed his son in vain and aborted God's plan.

> "And behold, the word of the LORD came to him (Abraham), saying, "This one shall not be your heir, but one (Isaac) who will come from your own body shall be your heir."
>
> **(Genesis 15:4)**

I have documented a lot of things God has said concerning my future, family, ministry, finances, etc. and when I spend time with God, the list expands more and more. I have come to understand that it's dangerous for me to assume I have reached God's final destination for my life, family and ministry. God is very strategic in His ways and this reflects in the way He reveals His plans to us.

The more we submit our lives to each fragment of His word, the more He reveals His prophetic agenda for our lives. When we refuse to submit, we become stranded in our pursuit of fulfilment.

2. Prophecy is Conditional

I once heard Dr. T.L Osborn say, "Covenants, promises and prophecies imply obligation, responsibility and rules". Every prophecy is conditional and this is one of the laws that governs prophecy. The law of condition must guide all prophecies in order for them to be fulfilled. No prophecy gets fulfilled without the recipient's involvement. Every promise from God requires our active partnership with Him for it to be realized. It is not God's idea to make His blessings for us difficult to reach, but to give us a sense of belonging as co-creators with Him.

Even though God told Adam in the 1st chapter of Genesis to be fruitful, He still expected him to tend the garden. Right from the beginning, God and man had been in the business of co-creating His desired plan on earth and this has not changed. God still co-creates with man! All through the Bible, when God proclaimed prophetic blessings upon an individual, a group of people or a nation, there were conditions attached to the blessing. God wants to give us an opportunity to be part of what He is doing in the earth.

Jesus Christ told Peter "follow me and I will make you fishers of men" (Matthew 4:19). Jesus' declaration over Peter hinted that his destiny would be to fish for men and become a great apostle, but the condition was for Peter to follow Jesus. All Peter needed to do was follow Christ and the rest was left for Jesus to make happen. By following Christ, Peter did become a great fisher of men, beginning with a great catch on the day of Pentecost (Acts 2).

If God says "arise and shine!" it means if you don't arise, you will not shine. It's not difficult to arise, is it? The truth is that God will never ask us to do what we can't do.

Whatever He wants us to do to connect to our blessings, He knows we can do. So, don't say "but God knows I can't". It's a lie from the pit of hell to rob you of fulfilment in your pursuit of success. Every promise from God comes with a condition and with every condition comes grace to obey.

In the book of Deuteronomy 28:3-13, we read God's prophecies of prosperity, protection, fruitfulness and influence over His children.

> "Blessed shall you be in the city, and blessed shall you be in the country.
>
> "Blessed shall be the fruit of your body, the produce of your ground and the increase of your herds, the increase of your cattle and the offspring of your flocks.
>
> "Blessed shall be your basket and your kneading bowl.
>
> "Blessed shall you be when you come in, and blessed shall you be when you go out.
>
> "The LORD will cause your enemies who rise against you to be defeated before your face; they shall come out against you one way and flee before you seven ways.
>
> "The LORD will command the blessing on you in your storehouses and in all to which you set your hand, and He will bless you in the land which the LORD your God is giving you. "The

LORD will establish you as a holy people to Himself, just as He has sworn to you, if you keep the commandments of the LORD your God and walk in His ways.

Then all peoples of the earth shall see that you are called by the name of the LORD, and they shall be afraid of you. And the LORD will grant you plenty of goods, in the fruit of your body, in the increase of your livestock, and in the produce of your ground, in the land of which the LORD swore to your fathers to give you.

The LORD will open to you His good treasure, the heavens, to give the rain to your land in its season, and to bless all the work of your hand. You shall lend to many nations, but you shall not borrow. And the LORD will make you the head and not the tail; you shall be above only, and not be beneath, if you heed the commandments of the LORD your God, which I command you today, and are careful to observe them."

(Deuteronomy 28:3–13)

Now, let us take particular note of the condition contained in verses 1 and 2:

"Now it shall come to pass, if you diligently obey the voice of the LORD your God, to observe carefully all His commandments which I command you today, that the LORD your God will set you high above all nations of the earth.

And all these blessings shall come upon you and overtake you, because you obey the voice of the LORD your God."

(Deuteronomy 28:1-2)

Here, God is teaching the law of condition. He says all of the prophetic declarations from verses 3 to 15 are subject to verses 1 and 2. The scriptures cannot be broken! It's time for the church to stop celebrating the promises of God alone and start obeying the conditions that will bring the promises to pass. We have too many preachers and very few doers! You can preach and still not be blessed but you can't obey God's instructions and not be blessed.

The law of motion says, "Every object remains at a state of rest until a force is applied." The same is true with prophecy. It remains unfulfilled until we apply ourselves to the conditions that activate its reality.

God's word is a seed and it is governed by certain principles for it to produce a harvest. Unless the conditions are fully met, the seed of God's word will remain unfruitful in our lives – a situation that will eventually lead to frustration and agony. I have learnt that if we do nothing with the word God speaks to us, the enemy, who knows the potential of God's word, will come and steal it away.

"The thief does not come except to steal, and to kill, and to destroy. I have come that they **may** have **life**, and that they **may** have it more abundantly."

(John 10:10)

For your blessing not to be stolen, act now!

3

The Power of The Prophetic

In Acts Chapter one, Jesus Christ specifically instructed His disciples not to move into what they had been called and trained to do until they were endued with POWER!

For anything or anyone to be an agent of change either positively or negatively, power is needed. Creation was birthed by the power of God. In Genesis 1, the presence of the Holy Spirit hovered over the surface of a formless earth and when God declared formation, change was inevitable.

> "In the beginning God created the heavens and the earth. The earth was without form, and void; and darkness was on the face of the deep. And the Spirit of God was hovering over the face of the waters.
>
> Then God said, "Let there be light"; and there was light. And God saw the light that it was good; and God divided the light from the darkness. God called the light Day and the darkness He called Night. So the evening and the morning were the first day. Then God said, "Let there be a firmament in the midst of the waters, and let it divide the waters from the waters."
>
> Thus God made the firmament, and divided the waters which were under the firmament from the waters which were above the firmament; and it

was so. And God called the firmament Heaven. So the evening and the morning were the second day.

Then God said, "Let the waters under the heavens be gathered together into one place, and let the dry land appear"; and it was so. And God called the dry land Earth, and the gathering together of the waters He called Seas. And God saw that it was good. Then God said, "Let the earth bring forth grass, the herb that yields seed, and the fruit tree that yields fruit according to its kind, whose seed is in itself, on the earth"; and it was so. And the earth brought forth grass, the herb that yields seed according to its kind, and the tree that yields fruit, whose seed is in itself according to its kind. And God saw that it was good. So the evening and the morning were the third day.

Then God said, "Let there be lights in the firmament of the heavens to divide the day from the night; and let them be for signs and seasons, and for days and years; and let them be for lights in the firmament of the heavens to give light on the earth"; and it was so. Then God made two great lights: the greater light to rule the day, and the lesser light to rule the night. He made the stars also. God set them in the firmament of the heavens to give light on the earth, and to rule over the day and over the night, and to divide the light from the darkness. And God saw that it was good. So the evening and the morning were the fourth day.

Then God said, "Let the waters abound with an abundance of living creatures, and let birds fly above the earth across the face of the firmament of the heavens." So God created great sea creatures and every living thing that moves, with which the waters abounded, according to their kind, and every winged bird according to its kind. And God saw that it was good. And God blessed them, saying, "Be fruitful and multiply, and fill the waters in the seas, and let birds multiply on the earth." So the evening and the morning were the fifth day.

Then God said, "Let the earth bring forth the living creature according to its kind: cattle and creeping thing and beast of the earth, each according to its kind"; and it was so. And God made the beast of the earth according to its kind, cattle according to its kind, and everything that creeps on the earth according to its kind. And God saw that it was good.

Then God said, "Let Us make man in Our image, according to Our likeness; let them have dominion over the fish of the sea, over the birds of the air, and over the cattle, over all the earth and over every creeping thing that creeps on the earth." So God created man in His own image; in the image of God He created him; male and female He created them.

Then God blessed them, and God said to them, "Be fruitful and multiply; fill the earth and subdue it; have dominion over the fish of the sea, over the birds of the air, and over every living thing that moves on the earth." And God said, "See, I have given you every herb that yields seed which is on the face of all the earth, and every tree whose fruit yields seed; to you it shall be for food.

Also, to every beast of the earth, to every bird of the air, and to everything that creeps on the earth, in which there is life, I have given every green herb for food"; and it was so. Then God saw everything that He had made, and indeed it was very good. So the evening and the morning were the sixth day."

(Genesis 1:1-31)

In the above passage, the presence of the Holy Spirit was an indication of God's power (ability) to create His desired change on earth.

How do I know this? In Acts 1:8 Jesus said,

"But you shall receive power when the Holy Spirit has come upon you; and you shall be witnesses to Me in Jerusalem, and in all Judea and Samaria, and to the end of the earth"

(Acts 1:8)

Luke 4:14 also says,

"Then Jesus returned in the power of the Spirit to Galilee, and news of Him went out through the entire surrounding region"

Without power, nothing changes! No prophetic word can change your life if it's not backed by the power-producing Spirit of the living God. In this chapter, we shall explore four power elements that validate a prophecy that is from God.

Divine Backing

Every prophetic word from God has the guarantee of God's backing or involvement. This implies that a prophetic word declared over your life has in it the ability (power) to bring God to the forefront of your life. No true prophecy excludes God because He is the one that will bring it to pass. Even though God requires your cooperation, He is still the Chief Executive Officer that will carry out His plan. Walking in God's word over your life delivers to you the power to have God on your side and if God be for you, who can be against you?

The Bible says Jesus looked at His disciples on a particular occasion and said to them,

> **"With men this is impossible, but with God all things are possible."**
>
> **(Matthew 19:26)**

I would like you to take a closer look at the above scripture. The word 'with' as used by Jesus in this statement is a profound word. The word means in agreement, in association, in partnership or in synergy. So, Jesus was saying in other words that when we synergize with men in the pursuit of our destiny, fulfilment in certain areas of our lives becomes unattainable. But, when we go into partnership with God, success and fulfilment are inevitable. Divine backing or divine partnership becomes easy when you locate God's word for your life, business or ministry.

A young man named Jeremiah received a prophetic word from God that he was predestined from his mother's womb to be a prophet to nations (Jeremiah 1:1-8). Unfortunately, Jeremiah did not seem to like the idea because he felt incapable of such an enormous task. God's response to Jeremiah's sincere confession of his incapability reveals something very important to the fulfilment of every man's destiny.

According to Jeremiah 1:6, Jeremiah had responded to God's prophetic word by saying, *"Ah, Lord God! Behold, I cannot speak, for I am a youth"*. I believe that Jeremiah was not trying to excuse himself from his divine responsibility but he was acknowledging the impossibility of achieving his divine task without a divine backing. A good observation of God's reply to Jeremiah's confession shows us that God wants to be there in our race to fulfilment. Here is what God said,

"Do not say,' I am a youth,' for you shall go to all
to whom I send you, and whatever I command
you, you shall speak. Do not be afraid of their
faces, for **I am with you** to deliver you," says
the Lord".

God shows us in this scripture that whatever He
commands of us, He will back. If there's a prophecy you are
running with at the moment, regardless of who spoke it, if it
does not put God on your side or God is not involved in it,
back off now! You can only embark on what God will back.
Psalm 126:1 says,

"Unless the Lord builds the house, they labor in
vain who build it; unless the Lord guards the city,
the watchman stays awake in vain".

And how does God create things? Through His words!

"In the beginning was the Word, and the Word
was with God, and the Word was God. He was
in the beginning with God. All things were made
through Him, and without Him nothing was
made that was made."

(John 1:1-3)

It is my prayer that you will not labour in vain in Jesus'
name. Amen.

Divine Direction

A Prophetic Word is like a spiritual satellite navigating system that gives us direction or tells us the way to go in our journey to fulfilling God's predestined plans for our future. A satellite navigator is common in developed countries. It is a device plugged to your car to give you direction to a des-ignated location. Having to travel on a one-thousand-mile journey without direction will end up in frustration.

A lot of people, including believers, are in this position of frustration today because they lack direction. When God created man, direction was one of the foremost things He sorted out because it wasn't His intention for man to struggle. God never created us to struggle in life. We struggle when we are disconnected from His plans for us or when we refuse to submit to the demands His will places on us.

Everyone created by God has a designated journey that can only be revealed by the one who assigns it and that person is God. When a prophetic word comes to you, it will come with direction. Some people say Abraham did not know where he was going when the word of God came to him to leave his father's house. That is true but God also told him to go "into a land that I will show you" (see Genesis 12:1).

Every prophetic word that gets you started and leaves you stranded is of the devil. Hear what God's word in Psalm 119:105 says *"Your word is a lamp to my feet and a light to my path"*. There is no way you will be stranded in the dark if you have light. Every time you believe false prophecies, darkness covers your destiny because it is a word from the master of darkness himself. This is not to put you in an uncomfortable position about prophets but to expose the evil device of the enemy so that you can discern those who speak over your life. Every prophecy from God will definitely bring light into your situation enabling you to see possibilities in your impossible situations and miracles in your obstacles.

I got a phone call one evening from a friend I had not heard from in a long time. We were not saved the last time we spoke and I was delighted to hear he had surrendered his heart to Jesus too. It was really a great reunion and we reminisced about old times together. Almost a week later, I got another call from him during which he shared his salvation experience and how he met a prophet who prophesied over his life. The shocking news was when he said that this prophet wanted me to get in touch with her because she had a word of prophecy for me. I thought to myself, "How in the world did she know me?" Then I asked my friend if there was any specific thing she said that I should know before calling her. According to him, the prophet said I needed to give my life to Christ and when I call more things will be revealed to me. At that point I could sense the spirit of deception; I knew this word was from the devil because I had given my life to Christ several years before then without any plans to take my life back from the Lord! I got very angry in my spirit and advised my friend to flee from false prophecies because I could sense the devil all over this arrangement.

It is ridiculous for anyone to prophesy that my name is Femi Adun, as I have borne the name since birth. Prophecy is not what I already know or have. It's a revelation of what is to be! I have come to learn that God does not prophesy into your past; He only prophesies into your future to shed light on your pathway to destiny.

In Matthew 1:21, Mary the mother of Jesus received a prophetic word from the Lord concerning the birth of her son. She could not have been confused about the destiny of the boy because it was clearly stated in the prophetic word:

> "And she will bring forth a Son, and you shall call His name Jesus, for He will save His people from their sins."
>
> **(Matthew 1:21)**

God will never speak to any man and leave him confused.

> "For God is not the author of confusion but of peace, as in all the churches of the saints."
>
> **(1 Corinthians 14:33)**

I pray that if you are in any confusion about God's plan for your life, you are delivered from every foul spirit of confusion right now in the name of Jesus Christ, Amen.

Divine Supply

Supernatural provision is an evidence of the presence of a prophetic involvement. God truly is a Great Provider but He only provides for what He has commanded.

The book of Lamentation 3:37 says:

> "Who is he who speaks (prophesies) and it comes to pass, when the Lord has not commanded (made provision for) it?"
>
> **(Lamentations 3:37)**

According to this scripture, when you run with a prophetic word that is either false or not meant for you, one of the outcomes you will experience is the lack of God's provision. You can rest assured that if God gives you a prophecy regarding your life, family, ministry or business, He will surely supply all the resources you need to accomplish it. I have never struggled to preach the word of God in any circumstance because I will always speak from the abundance of revelation He has put in my heart.   This is His divine provision validating His call on my life.   A true prophetic word will always bring about supernatural provision.

In 2 Kings 3, Jehoram the king of Israel accompanied by the king of Judah and the king of Edom went up to fight against the king of Moab.   After they had marched seven days through the route to Edom, they ran out of water for themselves and their animals. Then they called for Elisha the prophet who prophesied that there would be a supernatural supply of water and it came to pass almost immediately.

> "Now Jehoram the son of Ahab became king over Israel at Samaria in the eighteenth year of Jehoshaphat king of Judah, and reigned twelve years. And he did evil in the sight of the Lord, but not like his father and mother; for he put away the sacred pillar of Baal that his father had made. Nevertheless he persisted in the sins of Jeroboam the son of Nebat, who had made Israel sin; he did not depart from them. Now Mesha king of Moab was a sheep breeder, and he regularly paid the king of Israel one hundred thousand lambs and the wool of one hundred thousand rams. But it happened, when Ahab died, that the king of Moab rebelled against the king of Israel.

So King Jehoram went out of Samaria at that time and mustered all Israel. Then he went and sent to Jehoshaphat king of Judah, saying, "The king of Moab has rebelled against me. Will you go with me to fight against Moab?" And he said, "I will go up; I am as you are my people as your people, my horses as your horses." Then he said, "Which way shall we go up?" And he answered, "By way of the Wilderness of Edom." So the king of Israel went with the king of Judah and the king of Edom, and they marched on that roundabout route seven days; and there was no water for the army, or for the animals that followed them. And the king of Israel said, "Alas! For the LORD has called these three kings together to deliver them into the hand of Moab."

But Jehoshaphat said, "Is there no prophet of the Lord here that we may inquire of the LORD by him?" So one of the servants of the king of Israel answered and said, "Elisha the son of Shaphat is here, who poured water on the hands of Elijah." And Jehoshaphat said, "The word of the LORD is with him." So the king of Israel and Jehoshaphat and the king of Edom went down to him.

Then Elisha said to the king of Israel, "What have I to do with you? Go to the prophets of your father and the prophets of your mother." But the king of Israel said to him, "No, for the LORD has called these three kings together to deliver them into the hand of Moab." And Elisha said,

"As the LORD of hosts lives, before whom I stand, surely were it not that I regard the presence of Jehoshaphat king of Judah, I would not look at you, nor see you.

But now bring me a musician." Then it happened, when the musician played, that the hand of the LORD came upon him. And he said, "Thus says the LORD: 'Make this valley full of ditches.' For thus says the LORD: 'You shall not see wind, nor shall you see rain; yet that valley shall be filled with water, so that you, your cattle, and your animals may drink.'

And this is a simple matter in the sight of the LORD; He will also deliver the Moabites into your hand. Also you shall attack every fortified city and every choice city, and shall cut down every good tree, and stop up every spring of water, and ruin every good piece of land with stones." Now it happened in the morning, when the grain offering was offered, that suddenly water came by way of Edom, and the land was filled with water."

(2 Kings 3:1-20)

Along with a prophetic word comes divine supply, which is a sign to authenticate the word. The Bible says, *"he that receives a prophet shall receive a prophet's reward"* (Matthew 10:41). Supply is one of the rewards that emanate from embracing a prophetic covering. The reason for this is because prophecy, as I established in the first chapter, is the word of God and His word will always perform His will. Prophet Isaiah gave an insight about the nature of the word of God. He says:

> "So shall My word be that goes forth from My mouth; It shall not return to Me void, But it shall accomplish what I please, And it shall prosper in the thing for which I sent it."
>
> **(Isaiah 55:11)**

In 2006, the Lord told me to write, publish and launch my first book *The Seed,* but I said to myself at the time, "What would a dropout write? Where will I get finance to publish if at all I wrote something? How would I launch it?" This was where I began to learn about the power of the word God declares over us. In less than 6 months, all the three tasks were completed and fully paid for by God's divine provision. Glory to God!

Four years later the book is still in print blessing thousands of lives. It has travelled to many nations of the world and I have received endorsements of its impact by people in all walks of life. No matter how big your vision is, God gave it to you; hence the necessary resources to accomplish it can never be too much for Him. Plug into His divine plan and you will have uninterrupted access to divine supply.

God's word is an accomplisher of destiny. Each time it is released, the whole of heaven backs it up. Prophecies link us to the treasures of heaven and enable us to gain access to God's resources.

By the power of His word and in the name of Jesus Christ, I command resources to flow in your direction. Amen!

Divine Encouragement

For anyone to take delivery of what belongs to them in God's grand plan, there has to be courage, and sometimes we need encouragement to be courageous. The enemy will not just watch idly while you and I walk into our blessing. We will need to contend for what belongs to us and this is why it is important that we are encouraged.

Human beings can encourage you and not mean a word of it but when God does, something will surely lift inside of you. That is divine encouragement. It is important that we seek to be encouraged by God through His word. God encouraged Joshua before he embarked on the task of taking the children of Israel into the Promised Land:

> "Only be strong and very courageous, that you
> may observe to do according to all the law which

Moses My servant commanded you; do not turn
from it to the right hand or to the left, that you
may prosper wherever you go."

(Joshua 1:7)

Taking a closer look at the word of God to Joshua, 'only'
means 'one thing you must do.' The one thing each one of us
must do to conquer the enemy and take possession of our
blessings is to be strong in our courage, otherwise we have
no match against the enemy.

The word 'encourage' means 'to give confidence', which
then explains to us another vital role of a prophetic word in
our life. When the word of God comes in contact with your
own confidence, you become as bold as a lion. You are not
in fear of the future because you know what God has said or
is saying concerning your destiny. A student who has gotten
adequate information about a subject will not be afraid to be
tested on that particular topic. The same is true for everyone
who knows what God is saying about him/her.

Confidence is important to walk in the purposes of God
for our lives. We live in a society and world that threatens
and questions what we believe to be God's will for us. If we
are not confident of who God says we are, the world system
will pollute and discourage us from pursuing our dreams,
which is exactly what the enemy wants. The enemy wants
us, through a lack of confidence in God's word, to abandon

God's plans for our lives and begin to chase worldly ambitions. Don't be deceived. Rather, be encouraged. You carry something the world needs. The enemy knows this and is scared of you!

4

How to
Access and
Activate
The Prophetic

Prophecies, if they are not stirred up, can remain untapped. Prophecy must be accessed and activated for it to come alive. It is like an electric bulb that must be turned on for it to give light. The fact that you and I have a prophetic word over our lives is not enough. It is how well we can access and activate it that counts. Before any prophecy can be realized, it must first be accessed and activated. Here are a few keys on how to stir up the prophecies over your life in order for you to release the power in them.

Accept the need for a prophetic covering

The first step into your prophetic journey is to accept that God's word is essential to the success of anything you are doing. It is your need of it that opens the door for it. Without an expressive openness for a prophetic word, you may never receive one. God is very much interested in our success and He always wants to speak to us concerning our care. He doesn't have a problem giving us direction every time we need it, but most of us don't see or express our need for God's guidance via His word.

Let's take another close look at the experience of Jehoram, the king of Israel, with the other kings as recorded in 2 Kings 3. They faced a situation of drought without any solution but eventually found a way out of it. In verse 11, the Bible records that king Jehoshaphat said:

> "Is there no prophet of the LORD here that we may inquire of the LORD by him?" So one of the servants of the king of Israel answered and said, "Elisha the son of Shaphat is here, who poured water on the hands of Elijah."
>
> **(2 Kings 3:11)**

The kings, their men and all their animals would have died were it not for king Jehoshaphat acknowledging the need for a prophetic word from God concerning their ordeal. King Jehoshaphat displayed an understanding of the capability of God's word through His prophet. He knew God's prophetic word carries with it the capacity to super-naturally supply their need of water. There is no way their dehydrated soldiers could have won the war, so the supply of water was vital at that crucial moment. What this passage taught me is to seek God for His word in my times of trouble rather than murmur and complain as the king of Israel did,

"And the king of Israel said, "Alas! For the LORD
has called these three kings together to deliver
them into the hand of Moab."

(2 king 3:10)

I once had an experience that further strengthened my faith
in this important kingdom principle. Some time in the past,
God instructed me in the place of prayer to take three months
off from work for ministry purposes. I thought to myself,
"How on earth will my employer give me three months off
work, when it is clearly stated on my employment contract
that only three weeks leave was permitted at a time?" As
instructed by God, I went to inform the Administrative
department of my intention to go on three months' leave.
After a couple of weeks, I received an email from the head of
Admin informing me that I would need to write to the Chief
Executive Director for an approval of my request. As I read
the email, I knew there was a battle to fight or I might have to
put in my resignation letter knowing that my future lied in the
work of the ministry. However, I wrote the letter asking for
approval and sent it off with little hope (*by human standards*) of
my request being approved.

About two weeks later, I was preparing for a preaching
engagement when I found what appeared to be a prophetic
word for me from God's word. I was studying the book of
Nehemiah and how news came to him about the deplorable

state of the walls and gate of Jerusalem. After hearing these words, Nehemiah was grieved and prayed to God for favour before king Artaxerxes whom he served as a king's cupbearer.

Nehemiah prayed and went before the king and requested for permission to go and rebuild his fathers' land. Then the king asked Nehemiah how long he wanted to be gone for and Nehemiah set a time, *which was over 52 weeks leave from work*, and amazingly, the king granted Nehemiah's request. (See Nehemiah 1-3).

At this point, I was full of the Spirit. I received Nehemiah's testimony as a prophecy for myself. I even told my wife and a close friend that I had received a prophetic word from the Lord regarding my employer's approval of three months' leave and that I will still keep my job. After that revelation, I received a letter from my employer apologizing for the delay in getting back to me. He said that there had been a lot of deliberation on my case and that the Board of Directors had refused to let me go for that long since it is stated in my contract how much leave I can take per time. However, they were willing to compromise, that I should go and return to my job. I was not surprised because I already knew the power of the word God revealed to me.

One of the secrets to King David's outstanding and lasting success is embedded in this principle. He always sought the face of the Lord in every situation he found himself. David never felt too big to ask God for direction. Many people today put titles and offices before the word of God, forgetting that it is His word to us that makes our callings and titles relevant. David expressed his addiction to God's word throughout his writings. Little wonder God gave him all that he needed.

Dr. David Oyedepo of *The Living Faith Ministries* said, "Until you see wondrous things from the word of God, your life can never be wonderful". It is God's word in our lives that produces great and mighty deeds in and through us.

In John 5:24, Jesus Christ said:

> "I tell you the truth, whoever hears my word and believes in Him who sent Me has everlasting life, and shall not come into judgment, but has passed from death into life"
>
> **(John 5:24)**

Jesus Christ referred to Himself as a prophet.

> "He who receives you receives Me, and he who receives Me receives Him who sent Me. He who receives a prophet in the name of a prophet shall receive a prophet's reward. And he who receives a righteous man in the name of a righteous man shall receive a righteous man's reward."
>
> **(Matthew 10:40-41)**

In considering both scriptures, we can see that Jesus Christ is presenting us with an option to choose. If we accept the need for Him via His word, then we will cross over from death (not just physical death but all degradations of life) into Life (wealth and health). No matter what you are going through while reading this book, I urge you to turn to God, seek His face and He will surely send you a word.

Dr. Oyedepo has also said "This ministry will not be where it is today in terms of obvious and practical prosperity if what I heard God say to me at the inception of the ministry is what I am still running with". According to him, he goes back to God every now and then to get fresh revelation for the journey. We cannot afford to compromise hearing from God. Accepting the need for God's word in every situation of our life is as important as water is to a fish and oxygen to the human lungs.

Identify with a Prophet

After you accept the need for the prophetic word in your life, you then need to identify with a prophet. This is very important. When I say "identify with a prophet", I am not saying to be aware that someone is a prophet of God. No! It's deeper than that.

The book of 2 Kings 3 shows us that the kings who went to battle with King Jehoram accepted the need for a prophet when they were faced with their ordeal, but the situation did not just disappear because of their acceptance of the need of a prophet to bail them out. For their predicament to be resolved, they needed to recognize the position of a prophet in their situation and thank God one of the officers quickly came in to the rescue. He said *"Elisha son of Shaphat is here. He used to pour water on the hands of Elijah" (2 Kings 3:11b)*. The officer's rescue package would have remained a suggestion if the identification process was not completed, which is submission.

My great friend Gideon Mba, Senior Pastor of *Manifold International Church* once said, "One of the ways of activating or switching on the prophetic is through the law of recognition." This is an awesome truth!

In verse 12 of 2 Kings, the Bible records that King Jehoshaphat said *"The word of the LORD is with him"* and then he and the other kings went down to submit to Elisha the prophet. Going down to meet with Elisha completed that process of identification which led to their deliverance.

The principle of submission is a very important law all through the Bible. It's a spiritual principle that must not be ignored. Unfortunately, the spirit of pride has robbed this generation of its advantages and blessings. Another quote I like by Pastor Gideon Mba is, "Submission does not devalue you, it aligns you!" The devil wants to deny this generation of the fruit of submission by suggesting that to submit is to lose value. It is an absolutely lie from the pit of hell and a plan to rob us from God's best. There is nothing wrong with submission; it's the only way in God's kingdom to be elevated.

Today, young people in ministry don't want to identify with anybody. They want to run the race on their own and give all the glory to themselves. If you're one of these people, God's glory in your life is limited and will soon vanish.

We read in the Bible how Jesus Christ (*who, being in the form of God, did not consider it robbery to be equal with God*) submitted to John the Baptist (*a man*) to be baptized by him.

> "Then Jesus came from Galilee to John at the Jordan to be baptized by him. And John tried to prevent Him, saying, "I need to be baptized by You, and are You coming to me?" But Jesus answered and said to him, "Permit it to be so now, for thus it is fitting for us to fulfill all righteousness." Then he allowed Him. When He had been baptized, Jesus came up immediately from the water; and behold, the heavens were opened to Him, and He saw the Spirit of God descending like a dove and alighting upon Him. And suddenly a voice came from heaven, saying,

"This is My beloved Son, in whom I am well pleased."

(Matthew 3:13-17)

Dear friend, notice the argument between Jesus and John over who should baptize whom. In the spiritual order of things John the Baptist was in no way qualified to touch the strap sandal of Jesus, much less baptize Him.

"I indeed baptize you with water unto repentance, but He who is coming after me is mightier than I, whose sandals I am not worthy to carry. He will baptize you with the Holy Spirit and fire."

(Matthew 3:11)

Here are a few lessons from these verses of the scripture:

Never consider yourself too big to need help from others

We see Jesus Christ practise this principle in the above passage. Jesus was not just a great leader after John, but God Himself. The Bible says in Colossians 1:17 that *"And He (Jesus Christ) is before all things (including John the Baptist), and in Him (Jesus Christ) all things consist"*. Yet He submitted to John to be baptized by him because without the baptism, He could not be aligned to His destiny. As we read in the above scripture, the heavens opened and Jesus was declared the son of God that has come to deliver everyone at the river Jordan.

Don't question what God ordains

Jesus Christ could have questioned this whole arrangement but He did not. He said to John *"Permit it to be so now, for thus it is fitting for us to fulfil all righteousness".* Until we permit God's will, we can't submit to it which means we cannot fulfil it. Prophecy is God's will concerning His plans for our lives and we must submit to a requirement that governs it otherwise, there cannot be a fulfilment of that which is spoken by the Lord through His prophets.

If God decides you have to go through a particular minister to fulfil His call upon your life, then you better humble yourself and don't even try to figure or argue it out. That's what Jesus was trying to explain to John the Baptist and there was no point in arguing. Just as Jesus knew it was best for Him if John baptized Him, so also it is best for you and me if we submit ourselves to others ordained by God. I have always said to my colleagues in our ministry team that, "You can never say you have passed that test of humility until you serve someone who you are greater than by destiny or assignment."

Locate the person who is doing what you are called to do

To locate means, 'Take up residence and become established.' There are people who read other peoples' books, listen to their materials and will not publicly identify with them or even make an attempt to meet with them physically. The scriptures state that Jesus came from Galilee to John. Ensure you submit yourself to the prophet God ordains for you. Do not read their books only. It is good to read other peoples' books but if God has ordained a prophet over your life, it is important you meet that person physically.

Of course, you can learn from great men and women who have passed on to glory through their materials, but I'm talking about the ones that are alive. Remember in 2 Kings 3, the kings and his entourage went (physically) to meet Elisha the prophet. After I understood the power in this principle, I made up my mind that I will meet with the prophet God has placed over my life to receive God's word and impartation through him. I have done this in the last few years and I've got results to show for it, part of which you hold in your hands right now.

It is called mentoring or coaching in the business world, a powerful identification principle. Mentors function as 'modern prophets' who help to bring the future of your desire into the present and make it easy for you to access. They provide coverage and leverage for your business in order for you to avoid costly mistakes in the pursuit of success.

Coaching is very critical to the success of every business idea, as it provides guidance. Many people today underuse the power of technology due to a lack of guidance. When you buy a new technological device, it comes with an operation manual that needs to be read in order for its potentials to be fully maximized. The success of others who are ahead of you is a manual for your own future success and your success is a manual for others.

Prophet Elisha, who happened to be the saviour of the king and his army, identified (submitted) with a prophet. It was said of him: "...*Elisha the son of Shaphat is* here, *who poured water on the hands of Elijah*" *(2 Kings 3:11)*. Elisha's ability to carry out this exploit is connected to his relationship with another prophet. The easiest way for you to arrive at what God has spoken over your life is to walk with men or women who have already walked that path. There is a prepared way for every child of God to walk into their blessings and this way is prepared through men by God.

In the book of Ephesians 2:10 "*For we are His workmanship, created in Christ Jesus for good works, which God prepared beforehand that we should walk in them*".

Isaac Newton said, "If I have seen further it is by standing on the shoulders of giants". I am doing things today that I would never have imagined doing in my wildest dreams because God brought me in contact with my pastor and mentor, Sam Adeyemi (Pastor of *Daystar Christian Centre, Lagos Nigeria*). I have lost count of how many of his prophetic words over my life I am now walking in with obvious testimonies. I remember a particular prophetic prayer he prayed over me that God will collapse the future and then put it in my heart as a seed so that I can bring it to fruition. It was not too long after then that the Lord revealed to me the big picture of Grace House Int'l Ministry which is in full swing today.

When I was travelling to the United Kingdom for the first time, Pastor Sam prayed for me and said, "You will not just be a part of the system but you will transform the system". In less than two years, God honoured His word as declared by His servant and raised a platform where I lead people in the United Kingdom from all walks of life in praying for the nation to align with God's prophetic agenda. Signs and wonders are being documented from this gathering every month. Shortly after then, our ministry already established its first international based church in the heart of East London.

Friend, it is not only safe to identify with a prophet, it is rewarding! If you are not connected to anyone at the moment it's not too late to do so. You may be wondering, "How do I trust anyone?" The Bible says that by their fruit you will know them (*See Matthew 7:15*). Your prophet must have a prophet just like prophet Elisha poured water on Prophet Elijah's hand (*See 2 Kings 3:11*). Any prophet that cannot be connected to another person is a false prophet. Jesus Christ said, "As I see the father do, so do I" (*See John 5:30*). If the Bible states clearly that Jesus Christ had a father to reach out to, then no one's too big to have someone to look up to, including a prophet.

Pray and ask God to show you who He wants you to connect with and He will. Remember! In the school of impartation, connectivity is as vital as proximity!

Get connected and be lifted.

Believe in a prophet

Believing in the prophet God has placed over your life is very crucial to accessing the prophetic because the anointing we do not believe in will not work in our lives. You may wonder if this point is actually relevant, especially if you have already identified with a prophet. I will say yes! I have come across a lot of people who follow without believing.

They follow because they believe they have no choice or because others are following. Following is not enough to provoke the prophetic. Mere following is just like dancing around a ball - it will not get the ball between the goal posts. Just as a 'kicking force' is required to set the ball rolling, so is a 'believing force' required to access the prophetic.

Jesus Christ, the greatest and most powerful prophet of all times, was not just interested in a 'following crowd'. He spent more time with the people who believed in Him. It wasn't that He wanted to boost His ego by having a multitude of people following or believing in Him, No! It is because He wants everybody to know that no one can get anything from Him except by believing.

God is the one who works through a prophet and the Bible says, "Without faith it is impossible to please God". In other words when we believe in the prophet over our lives, we are not only believing the man of God, we are exercising our faith in God and when this happens, God releases His word concerning our situation which in turn will get rid of every obstacle to our success.

"Jesus said to him, *If you can believe, all things are possible to him who believes.*" (Mark 9:23)

In the latter part of 2 Chronicles 20:20, the Bible says "Believe in the Lord your God, and you shall be established;

believe His prophets, and you shall prosper". God has deliberately tied some of our prosperity to prophets He places over lives. Of course, not just anybody can be a prophet over your life. There is a God-ordained man or woman that will decree God's promise over your life and it will come to pass. In the above scripture, we can see that even though it is non-negotiable to believe in God, we must also believe in prophets so we can access the blessings of God for our lives through prophetic declarations.

I have never had a reason to doubt the teaching or declarations of my pastor. What I have become today has made it too late for me to doubt anything he has said. I am so blessed to have submitted my life to God's grace and anointing upon his life, family and ministry to the extent that I have become a channel of blessing and hope to bless thousands of people across the nations. The day you begin to doubt or argue with what your prophet is saying is the day you begin to lose the benefits that flow to you from him, and if nothing flows to you, nothing flows from you. It is simple − you cannot give what you don't have! Your pastor or mentor may not need anything from you, but you will always need to receive from your pastor or mentor such as his/her anointing, wisdom or experience in order for you to impact others. I say this because some people develop a bad attitude towards their mentors. But this is wrong. You are important because you have the privilege of being a protégée.

In Luke 1, Elizabeth was moved by the Spirit of God and she declared to Mary the mother of Jesus that *"Blessed is she who believed, for there will be a fulfilment of those things which were told her from the Lord"* (Luke 1:39- 41). There is no performance until you believe. For you and me to experience the promises of God over our lives, there must be an unwavering faith and commitment to God's word as declared by His prophet.

Do not allow the devil to rob you. One of the ways he does this is to destroy your faith (*The thief does not come except to steal, and to kill, and to destroy... John 10:10). The devil wants to steal y*our 'belief system' by throwing all sorts of overwhelming challenges at you. Once he can successfully do this, he knows your chances of seeing the fulfilment of God's word over your life are slim. The enemy wants you to think and confess that nothing good can happen to you anymore. But the good news is that when Jesus died on the cross, our challenges were converted and made to validate the prophecy over our lives and not to negate it. Concerning Jesus Christ Himself, the Bible stated that *"if the rulers of this age had known, they would not have crucified Jesus" (1 Corinthians 2:8)*. Now, the reason for this is because the enemy did not know that the glorification of Christ was in His crucifixion. If he had known this, he would have kept Him alive. Glory to God that Christ was crucified!

The same still obtains with you and me today. Anytime the enemy strikes at us, he is just activating the promises of God over our lives. Just like he was ignorant of the fact that the more he challenged Jesus, the more he was pushing Him into His destiny. In the same vein, he does not know that every challenging situation he throws at you is only pushing you closer to the prophetic agenda of God for your life. Isn't it a relief to know that all things work together for good to those who love God and are called according to His purpose (Romans 8:28)? So be at peace and believe that things are working out as declared by God's chosen prophet over your life.

Give to your prophet

There are different ways by which you can give to a prophet God has placed over your life. These include your prayers, giving open credits to him/her where necessary, honouring them with your words and deeds and giving financial or material gifts to them. Your giving to a prophet does not make him/her blessed; you are the one who gets blessed by giving. Our giving to God is to make us richer and blessed and not to make Him richer or more blessed. No one can make God richer! After all, all silver and gold are His.

"The silver is Mine, and the gold is Mine", says the LORD of hosts.

(Haggai 2:8)

For God to raise someone up as a prophet makes that person a blessed man/woman already and they are blessed to be a blessing, not a beggar! Stop treating men of God like beggars by thinking they need money or anything else from you. You are the one who will wallow in lack if you don't give to them. Here's what the Bible says in Hebrews 7:7,

"Now beyond all contradiction the lesser is blessed by the better."

(Hebrews 7:7)

This word of the Lord says beyond all disagreement or opposition to this all-time spiritual principle for living a life of abundance, the lesser is going to be blessed by the better. This has been and will always be. Men and women have come and gone but the word of the Lord has remained. We saw clearly in 2 Kings 3:11 how it is said that Elisha poured water on Elijah's hand.

"But Jehoshaphat said, "Is there no prophet of the LORD here that we may inquire of the LORD by him?" So one of the servants of the king of Israel answered and said, "Elisha the son of Shaphat is here, who poured water on the hands of Elijah."

(2 Kings 3:11)

Elijah did not need the anointing on Elisha; it was Elisha that wanted a double portion of Elijah's anointing and he got it by giving everything up to connect with it.

"And so it was, when they had crossed over, that Elijah said to Elisha, "Ask! What may I do for you, before I am taken away from you?" Elisha said, "Please let a double portion of your spirit be upon me."

(2 Kings 2:9)

It had been prophesied that Elisha would become God's mighty prophet but he needed the grace of God on another man's life (Elijah) to come into the fullness of what was spoken concerning him:

"Also you shall anoint Jehu the son of Nimshi as king over Israel. And Elisha the son of Shaphat of Abel Meholah you shall anoint as prophet in your place. 17 It shall be that whoever escapes the sword of Hazael, Jehu will kill; and whoever escapes the sword of Jehu, Elisha will kill."

(1 Kings 19:16-17)

Elisha had a great destiny but not without a committed giving relationship to Elijah, his God-ordained prophet. Apostle Paul taught the Corinthian church this principle.

"If we have sown spiritual things for you, is it a
great thing if we reap your material things?"

(I Corinthians 9:11)

It is important that we give to those who minister
spiritual blessings to us. In order not to cut the flow of the
spiritual blessings coming into our lives through the prophet
of God, we need to constantly service the channel it flows
through by giving gifts of any form (not just monetary gifts).
We give up to go up, because what we give to God's
prophet is a seed and in that seed, there is capacity to
multiply what comes back to you which is your harvest.

In the book of 1 Samuel chapter 9, we learnt that a young
lad called Saul with a servant of his father, went on a rescue
mission to find his father's donkeys that got lost. Having
searched for quite a while, they still could not find the
missing donkeys. His servant who had been searching with
him suggested they go and inquire from a prophet as it was
the custom back then. In verse 7, Saul asked a question that
is worth paying attention to. He said "But look, if we go,
what shall we bring the man? For the bread in our vessels is
all gone, and there is no present to bring to the man of God.
What do we have?" In verse 8, Saul's servant answered and
said "Look, I have here at hand one-forth of a shekel of
silver. I will give that to the man of God, to tell us our way".

I will like to draw your attention to two important truths from this passage of the Bible. Firstly, you don't have to give only monetary gift to a man of God, for Saul did not say "we don't have money", what he said is "we don't have any bread left", signifying that a gift to a man of God should not only be money. Secondly, giving to a man of God is scriptural and vital for every believer to connect to the wisdom of God through the office or ministry of a prophet.

This principle of giving to your prophet is not a man-made idea to rip people off; it is a biblical truth for you as a child of God to connect to heaven's treasure for an enviable life on earth - regardless of false prophets and so-called ministers of the gospel who have taken advantage of vulnerable and immature Christians.

In the book of Mark 14:3, there was a woman whose story has become a popular sermon in the church of God. She poured a very costly bottle of perfumed oil on Jesus Christ's head. Many who were present wondered why she poured such expensive oil on Him like that. Some even suggested she could have sold it and then brought the money, but Jesus shut all of them up knowing that she would receive a far more excellent and greater reward than the oil. Today as Jesus decreed, her story has been read by millions of people in numerous languages across nations all over the world.

Let me draw a balance here now in concluding this chapter. You don't have to get into any trouble or pressure to give to a man of God. You are only sowing a seed, and usually seeds are not as big as their fruits. The truth is that you can still touch God's heart with the little you have. No one should be under any pressure to give. You do not need to sow a tree to reap a harvest. No! It will only take a couple of seeds to produce a tree and as your fruits increase, you can increase your seeds.

5

Hindrances
To
Prophecy

In this chapter, I will like to draw our attention to three major hindrances to the fulfilment of God's word over us. The Bible refers to the word of God as seeds and the human heart as the soil where the seed will be planted. Now, if a seed planted in the soil is not properly cultivated, the growth of such a seed may be stunted or hindered by weeds. The same is true with prophecy - it can be hindered from coming to pass by what I call 'prophecy hindrances'. Let's consider them below.

Hindrance 1: Sin

Birds are one of the most blessed creatures God made, especially with their ability to fly. The eagle is unique among birds, with so many great attributes that are applicable to some of the success elements or qualities of the human being. It is said that the eagle is a creature of swiftness, strength, courage, wisdom, keen sight (vision), intuition and creativity.

From the eagle eye, we learn that life looks different from an aerial perspective. Through its connection to the air element, the eagle is connected to intelligence, but also to the spirit (supernatural realm). Some of the eagle's powers are independence, vision and strength. The eagle's vision is 8 times stronger than the human's, enabling him to see prey miles off. Weighing less than a domestic cat, the eagle's strength has nothing to do with his size. His feet and talons are stronger than a human hand, able to soar down with precision grabbing hold of the prey, mid-flight.

Now, you may be wondering what this has to do with hindrance to prophecy. It has everything to do with it! Of what benefit are all of the eagle's strengths if it's caught by a snare and thrown in a cage forever? Have a think about it! God deliberately put all of these powerful elements in the eagle for it to fulfil its destiny with style and splendour but all of these will be aborted once an eagle is trapped in a cage. Sin is a snare (cage) that traps us in order to abort our glorious and majestic destiny in God. In the book of Genesis, God created man (male and female) with limitless potential and power to rule and enjoy all-round success.

> "Then God said, "Let Us make man in Our image, according to Our likeness; let them have dominion over the fish of the sea, over the birds of the air, and over the cattle, over all the earth and over every creeping thing that creeps on the earth." So God created man in His own image; in the image of God He created him; male and female He created them.

Then God blessed them, and God said to them, "Be fruitful and multiply; fill the earth and subdue it; have dominion over the fish of the sea, over the birds of the air, and over every living thing that moves on the earth." And God said, "See, I have given you every herb that yields seed which is on the face of all the earth, and every tree whose fruit yields seed; to you it shall be for food.

Also, to every beast of the earth, to every bird of the air, and to everything that creeps on the earth, in which there is life, I have given every green herb for food"; and it was so. Then God saw everything that He had made, and indeed it was very good. So the evening and the morning were the sixth day."

(Genesis 1:26-31)

All of these were not possible the very moment man (male and female) became exposed to sin.

"Now the serpent was more cunning than any beast of the field which the LORD God had made. And he said to the woman, "Has God indeed said, 'You shall not eat of every tree of the garden?" And the woman said to the serpent, "We may eat the fruit of the trees of the garden; but of the fruit of the tree which is in the midst of the garden, God has said, 'You shall not eat it, nor shall you touch it, lest you die." Then the serpent said to the woman, "You will not surely die.

For God knows that in the day you eat of it your eyes will be opened and you will be like God, knowing good and evil." So when the woman saw that the tree was good for food, that it was pleasant to the eyes, and a tree desirable to make one wise, she took of its fruit and ate. She also gave to her husband with her, and he ate. Then the eyes of both of them were opened, and they knew that they were naked; and they sewed fig leaves together and made themselves coverings.

And they heard the sound of the Lord God walking in the garden in the cool of the day, and Adam and his wife hid themselves from the presence of the LORD God among the trees of the garden. Then the Lord God called to Adam and said to him, "Where are you?" So he said, "I heard Your voice in the garden, and I was afraid because I was naked; and I hid myself." And He said, "Who told you that you were naked? Have you eaten from the tree of which I commanded you that you should not eat?" Then the man said, "The woman whom You gave to be with me, she gave me of the tree, and I ate."

And the LORD God said to the woman, "What is this you have done?" The woman said, "The serpent deceived me, and I ate." So the LORD God said to the serpent: "Because you have done this, you are cursed more than all cattle, and more than every beast of the field; on your belly you shall go, and you shall eat dust all the days of your life.

And I will put enmity between you and the woman, and between your seed and her Seed; He shall bruise your head, and you shall bruise His heel." To the woman He said: "I will greatly multiply your sorrow and your conception; in pain you shall bring forth children; your desire shall be for your husband, and he shall rule over you." Then to Adam He said, "Because you have heeded the voice of your wife, and have eaten from the tree of which I commanded you, saying, 'You shall not eat of it': "Cursed is the ground for your sake; in toil you shall eat of it all the days of your life. Both thorns and thistles it shall bring forth for you, and you shall eat the herb of the field.

In the sweat of your face you shall eat bread till you return to the ground, for out of it you were taken; for dust you are, And to dust you shall return." And Adam called his wife's name Eve, because she was the mother of all living. Also for Adam and his wife the Lord God made tunics of skin, and clothed them. Then the Lord God said, "Behold, the man has become like one of Us, to know good and evil. And now, lest he put out his hand and take also of the tree of life, and eat, and live forever", therefore the Lord God sent him out of the garden of Eden to till the ground from which he was taken. So He drove out the man;

and He placed cherubim at the east of the
garden of Eden, and a flaming sword which
turned every way, to guard the way to the tree
of life."

(Genesis 3:1-22)

Sin is a major hindrance to the fulfilment of God's
promise concerning our future. There is no limit to what we
can achieve in life but when sin is present, the future
becomes bleak. Living a sinful life is like an eagle living in a
cage; it traps your potential to live a successful life created
for you by God. Many Christians live a life short of God's
blessing because of this reason - sin. Adam and Eve were so
blessed but they gave it all up to sin.

The devil will look for every means to make us fall short
of God's blessing by presenting evil as good. We see all
around us today how the media sells evil to us as good,
through explicit videos and pictures dressed up as 'freedom
of expression', promotion of alcoholism, promotion of safe
sex as best sex. All these are devices of the devil to get God's
precious children trapped. The Bible instructs us not to be
ignorant of the devices of the devil so that we do not fall for
his temptations.

A cage does not change an eagle into a rat; it only
undermines its potentials. So also, sin cannot change God's
plan for your future, it only hinders you from reaching the

fullness of God's plans and blessing for you. Nothing changes the mind of God concerning us. The devil has no power over our destiny except through sin. For this reason we must fight the war against sin. The good news is that the battle is already decided in our favour if we are born again as Jesus Christ already won the war on our behalf at Calvary. Hallelujah! We are delivered from the life of sin and made just by grace through faith in Jesus Christ.

> "But now the righteousness of God apart from the law is revealed, being witnessed by the Law and the Prophets, even the righteousness of God, through faith in Jesus Christ, to all and on all who believe. For there is no difference; for all have sinned and fall short of the glory of God, being justified freely by His grace through the redemption that is in Christ Jesus, whom God set forth as a propitiation by His blood, through faith, to demonstrate His righteousness, because in His forbearance God had passed over the sins that were previously committed, to demonstrate at the present time His righteousness, that He might be just and the justifier of the one who has faith in Jesus."
>
> **(Romans 3:21-26)**

See what another translation says;

"But in our time something new has been added. What Moses and the prophets witnessed to all those years has happened. The God-setting-things -right that we read about has become Jesus-setting-things-right for us. And not only for us, but for everyone who believes in him. For there is no difference between us and them in this, since we've compiled this long and sorry record as sinners (both us and them) and proved that we are utterly incapable of living the glorious lives God wills for us, God did it for us. Out of sheer generosity he put us in right standing with himself. A pure gift! He got us out of the mess we're in and restored us to where he always wanted us to be. And he did it by means of Jesus Christ.

God sacrificed Jesus on the altar of the world to clear that world of sin. Having faith in him sets us in the clear. God decided on this course of action in full view of the public to set the world in the clear with himself through the sacrifice of Jesus, finally taking care of the sins he had so patiently endured. This is not only clear, but it's now this is current history! God sets things right. He also makes it possible for us to live in his rightness."

(Romans 3:21-26 The Message)

Praise God! Christ is our Redeemer. The Bible makes it clear that after the fall of Adam and Eve, man's redemption can only be found in Christ.

"You know the story of how Adam landed us in the dilemma we're in first sin, then death, and no one exempt from either sin or death. That sin disturbed relations with God in everything and everyone, but the extent of the disturbance was not clear until God spelled it out in detail to Moses. So death, this huge abyss separating us from God, dominated the landscape from Adam to Moses. Even those who didn't sin precisely as Adam did by disobeying a specific command of God still had to experience this termination of life, this separation from God. But Adam, who got us into this, also points ahead to the One who will get us out of it.

Yet the rescuing gift is not exactly parallel to the death-dealing sin. If one man's sin put crowds of people at the dead-end abyss of separation from God, just think what God's gift poured through one man, Jesus Christ, will do! There's no comparison between that death-dealing sin and this generous, life-giving gift. The verdict on that one sin was the death sentence; the verdict on the many sins that followed was this wonderful life sentence. If death got the upper hand through one man's wrongdoing, can you imagine the breathtaking recovery life makes, sovereign life, in those who grasp with both hands this wildly extravagant life-gift, this grand setting-everything-right that the one man Jesus Christ provides?

Here it is in a nutshell: Just as one person did it wrong and got us in all this trouble with sin and death, another person did it right and got us out of it. But more than just getting us out of trouble, he got us into life! One man said no to God and put many people in the wrong; one man said yes to God and put many in the right.

All that passing laws against sin did was produce more lawbreakers. But sin didn't, and doesn't, have a chance in competition with the aggressive forgiveness we call grace. When it's sin versus grace, grace wins hands down. All sin can do is threaten us with death, and that's the end of it. Grace, because God is putting everything together again through the Messiah, invites us into life a life that goes on and on and on, world without end."

(Romans 5:12-21 The Message)

Glory to God! There is a way and that way is through Jesus Christ. All we need is to confess our sins and receive Him as Saviour of our lives and right away, we'll begin to live the life He intended for us.

"But what does it say? "The word is near you, in your mouth and in your heart" (that is, the word of faith which we preach): that if you confess with your mouth the Lord Jesus and believe in your heart that God has raised Him from the dead, you will be saved. For with the heart one believes unto righteousness, and with the mouth confession is made unto salvation."

(Romans 10:8-10)

The word 'saved' in the above scripture is from the Greek word 'Sozo' meaning salvation, healing and deliverance. When we give our lives to Jesus, we experience all three. We are not just born again but we are healed of every disease and sickness as well as being delivered from every form of oppression from the devil.

I challenge you now; the word is in your mouth. Will you dare to believe and confess your sins before Jesus your Saviour? If you will, then join me in confessing these words:

"Dear Lord Jesus, I confess that I have sin and I believe you have taken away my sins when You died on the cross. I believe you are raised from the dead, so therefore I accept You as my Lord and Saviour forever, Amen."

Friend, I congratulate you. You are now restored to the path of righteousness where the fulfilment of God's promise to you is guaranteed.

"Strengthening the souls of the disciples, exhorting them to continue in the faith, and saying, "We must through many tribulations enter the kingdom of God."

(Act 14:22)

Hindrance 2: Unbelief

Another great enemy of prophecy is unbelief. No matter how great and colourful your destiny is, without faith you can never take delivery of it. Whatever God declared over you by prophecy requires you to believe it will come to pass otherwise you may hinder it altogether. Unbelief is like cancer that eats up one's destiny. Prophecy is God's promise concerning our future and it will demand our faith to obtain it. The Bible says we should imitate those who through faith and patience inherit the promise (Hebrews 6:12). Faith is the currency we exchange for a glorious future. Delay is a product of unbelief, even though no one can change God's plan for your life, the reality of God's plan for you can be delayed through your unbelief.

It was never God's intention to keep the Israelites in the wilderness for 40 years before bringing them into the Promised Land. It was unbelief that led them to disobeying God, and that made their stay in the wilderness longer than it should have been. All through the Bible, we would see several cases of unbelief and consequences of it.

Here are some cases of unbelief in the word of God:

In 2 Kings 7:1-2, there was a great and terrible recession in Israel and the word of the Lord came through Prophet

Elisha to the king of Israel concerning the economic situation of his land. God's word came to the king that in 24 hours, the economic chaos will be reverted and things will become surplus again.

> "Then Elisha said, "Hear the word of the LORD. Thus says the LORD: 'Tomorrow about this time a seah (measure) of fine flour shall be sold for a shekel and two seahs (measure) of barley for a shekel, at the gate of Samaria."
>
> **(2 Kings 1:1)**

Now, this was great and relieving news to the king and his people. The word eventually came to pass because the word of God does not fail.

> "Then the people went out and plundered the tents of the Syrians. So a seah (measure) of fine flour was sold for a shekel and two seahs (measure) of barley for a shekel, according to the word of the LORD."
>
> **(2 Kings 7:16)**

Everyone in the land had more than enough to purchase what they wanted with a very little amount of money according to the prophecy. Only one man did not live long enough to enjoy the spoils because of unbelief. This man was one of the king's officers present at the time prophet Elisha declared the word of God to the king. When the prophet said that there was going to be a miracle in the land overnight, this man responded in unbelief and doubted if this could really happen.

> "So an officer on whose hand the king leaned answered the man of God and said, "Look, if the LORD would make windows in heaven, could this thing be?" And he said, "In fact, you shall see it with your eyes, but you shall not eat of it."
>
> **(2 Kings 7:2)**

True to God's word, the officer saw the miracle but did not eat of it.

> "Now the king had appointed the officer on whose hand he leaned to have charge of the gate. But the people trampled him in the gate, and he died, just as the man of God had said, who spoke when the king came down to him."
>
> **(2 kings 7:17)**

Friend, unbelief does not change God's plan for your life but hinders you from partaking in its reality. God's word concerning Israel came to pass in spite of the officer's unbelief, only that he was cut off from it. Unbelief cuts us off from God's plan for our future; it is Satan's device of hindering us from getting our glorious and colourful future in God.

In the book of Matthew 13, scriptures reveal that even though Jesus was willing, he could not do many mighty works (miracles) in His native land, Nazareth, because of the people's unbelief. *(Matthew 13:58)*

Everything God has is for us His children but there is no way we will have access to them if we constantly doubt His word either written or spoken. Unbelief is what the devil says concerning you or God's word for you, and this is always in opposition to prosperity and blessings. The force to combat unbelief is the force of God's word.

> **"So then faith comes by hearing, and hearing by the word of God."**
>
> **(Romans 10:17)**

Friend, it time to kick out every form of unbelief in your way by getting into the word of God and pulling out what God says you are and not what Satan wants you to believe. Get going now!

Hindrance 3: Pride

Another hindrance to working in the reality of God's promise over your life is pride. Pride is as deadly as venom; it drains God's grace out of your effort to fulfilling God's plan for your future and makes it more difficult to realizing it. God detests pride and will not have anything to do with a proud person. His word says, *"He resists the proud"* (James 4:6).

The office of a prophet is not some place anyone can occupy by a college or university degree. Prophets are ordained by God and they can be anybody, of any age and from any culture. You will only rob yourself of the grace of God to fulfil your destiny in a grand style if you feel someone is too young/old, different from your race or inadequate in one way or the other to prophesy over your life. Only proud people feel that way and they may never derive any benefit from the ministry of a prophet.

Naaman, commander of the army of the king of Syria almost missed the benefit of the ministry of the prophet because of pride according to 2 Kings 5. The Bible describes Naaman as a great and honourable man before the king of Syria because by him God had given victory to Syria. He was also a mighty man of valour but there was one thing about him that didn't represent honour - Naaman was a leper! Naaman with all of the accolades needed something more important i.e. healing. Leprosy is not something nice. It is a terrible thing to have because people who had the condition in the old days were considered to be outcast. Here's the account of Naaman's story in the Bible:

> "Now Naaman, commander of the army of the king of Syria was a great and honorable man in the eyes of his master, because by him the LORD had given victory to Syria. He was also a

mighty man of valor, but a leper. And the Syrians
had gone out on raids, and had brought back
captive a young girl from the land of Israel. She
waited on Naaman's wife. Then she said to her
mistress, "If only my master were with the
prophet who is in Samaria! For he would heal
him of his leprosy." And Naaman went in and
told his master, saying, "Thus and thus said the
girl who is from the land of Israel." Then the king
of Syria said, "Go now, and I will send a letter to
the king of Israel." So he departed and took with
him ten talents of silver, six thousand shekels of
gold, and ten changes of clothing.

Then he brought the letter to the king of Israel,
which said, Now be advised, when this letter
comes to you, that I have sent Naaman my
servant to you, that you may heal him of his
leprosy. And it happened, when the king of Israel
read the letter, that he tore his clothes and said,
"Am I God, to kill and make alive, that this man
sends a man to me to heal him of his leprosy?
Therefore please consider, and see how he seeks
a quarrel with me." So it was, when Elisha the
man of God heard that the king of Israel had
torn his clothes that he sent to the king saying,
"Why have you torn your clothes? Please let him
come to me, and he shall know that there is a
prophet in Israel."

Then Naaman went with his horses and chariot,
and he stood at the door of Elisha's house. And

Elisha sent a messenger to him, saying, "Go and wash in the Jordan seven times, and your flesh shall be restored to you, and you shall be clean." But Naaman became furious, and went away and said, "Indeed, I said to myself, 'He will surely come out to me, and stand and call on the name of the LORD his God, and wave his hand over the place, and heal the leprosy.' Are not the Abanah and the Pharpar, the rivers of Damascus, better than all the waters of Israel? Could I not wash in them and be clean?" So he turned and went away in a rage. And his servants came near and spoke to him, and said, "My father, if the prophet had told you to do something great, would you not have done it? How much more then, when he says to you, 'Wash, and be clean'?" So he went down and dipped seven times in the Jordan, according to the saying of the man of God; and his flesh was restored like the flesh of a little child, and he was clean."

(2 Kings 5:1-14)

Regardless of the great reputation he had, Naaman would have remained a leper for the rest of his life if he did not humble himself and obey the instructions of Prophet Elisha. No matter your reputation, you must humble yourself at all times or you may never enjoy the grace of God on His Prophets. The Bible says that "God comes in the cool of the day to fellowship with Adam". If God can come down to man's level, then what is man to man? This was the same mind that was in Jesus - He didn't mind giving up His godly nature and coming in the form of man.

Humility was one of the foremost character qualities that Jesus displayed in His pursuit of prophecy. John the Baptist had prophesied about Jesus Christ coming and baptizing people with fire, a much greater ministry than his. But when Jesus finally showed up, He didn't just go into the ministry because His destiny was greater and more supreme than anyone else's. The Bible records that Jesus went and submitted Himself for John the Baptist to baptize Him with water when He, by destiny, will baptize with fire and the Holy Spirit. Isn't that great humility?

"Then Jesus came from Galilee to John at the Jordan to be baptized by him. And John tried to prevent Him, saying, "I need to be baptized by You, and are You coming to me?" But Jesus answered and said to him, "Permit it to be so now, for thus it is fitting for us to fulfill all righteousness." Then he allowed Him. When He had been baptized, Jesus came up immediately from the water; and behold, the heavens were opened to Him, and He saw the Spirit of God descending like a dove and alighting upon Him. And suddenly a voice came from heaven, saying, "This is My beloved Son, in whom I am well pleased."

(Matthew 3:13-17)

In the Scripture above, there was an argument between John and Jesus on who to baptize whom because both of these great men understood the law of recognition. In my opinion, there are two levels of humility in this passage.

Humility to a higher Authority

The first level of humility is the humility to a higher authority. This dimension of humility could be questioned but vital to the fulfilment of your future via the ministry of a prophet. God wants us to humble ourselves and learn from those who are ahead of us in order to make our journey to success easily attainable. No matter how much you and I know, experience has an advantage over knowledge. I believe Jesus understood this

This is a lesson to all of us hoping to do something great in the future. No matter what you will be baptizing people with, you still need to learn how to do it. On one hand, it was easy for John to be humbled before Jesus knowing that Jesus wasn't just a great leader but God Himself in human form (see Philippians 2:7). Most times when we claim humility, we do so because it is easier for us to humble ourselves before someone superior to us in whatever form. Superiority shouldn't be the only reason for our humility but genuine submission and openness of heart.

Humility to a Lower Authority

This dimension of humility has much impact and blessing on us in our journey in life. There is one man I know that constantly lived His life by this level of humility and that person is Jesus Christ. Jesus humbled Himself before higher authorities but much more to people of lower authority than His. He was conscious of this as we see in the Scriptures.

The Holy Spirit once spoke to me that until I am able to serve someone who (based on revelation) by destiny I am greater than, I cannot claim that I am humble. You may wonder if this is scriptural. Yes! In fact it is the biblical requirement for any believer who wants to enjoy God's grace. Jesus is the word (John 1) and all things were created by Him including John the Baptist, yet He could still humble Himself to be baptized by someone He created. This kind of humility is scarce in the church of God today.

> "Let nothing be done through selfish ambition or conceit, but in lowliness of mind let each esteem others better than himself. Let each of you look out not only for his own interests, but also for the interests of other "Let this mind be in you which was also in Christ Jesus, who, being in the form of God, did not consider it robbery to be equal with God, but made Himself of no reputation, taking the form of a bondservant, and

coming in the likeness of men. And being found in appearance as a man, He humbled Himself and became obedient to the point of death, even the death of the cross."

(Philippians 2:3-8)

Also in 1 Peter 5:5, the bible says,

Likewise you younger people, submit yourselves to your elders. Yes, **all of you** be submissive to one another, and be clothed with humility, for "GOD RESISTS THE PROUD, BUT GIVES GRACE TO THE HUMBLE."

(1 Peter 5:5 emphasis mine)

I pray that this level of humility will be found in the body of Christ today, that we will stop seeing ourselves as better than others and that we will serve everyone with love and equality. Amen!

6

*Operating
And Growing
in the Prophetic*

Over a period of time, I have often heard Rev. Lekan Fasina, Senior Pastor of *Ignite Churches International*, and founder of *Treasures in Clay International* say, "Everyone is prophetic to a degree". You and I can operate and grow in the prophetic. In the book of John 16, Jesus Christ teaches that it is possible for believers to operate in the prophetic without necessarily being called into the office of a prophet (Ephesians 4:11) through the help of the Holy Spirit.

> "I have much more to say to you, more than you can now bear. But when he, the Spirit of truth comes, he will guide you into all truth. He will not speak on his own; he will speak only what he hears, and he will tell you what is yet to come. He will bring glory to me by taking from what is mine and making it known to you. All that belongs to the Father is mine. That is why I said the Spirit will take from what is mine and make it known to you."
>
> **(John 16:12-15)**

Prophecy is futuristic i.e. what is to come, and the Holy Spirit according to Jesus is assigned to bring to our knowledge those things that God has for our future. What I like about these statements made by Jesus is that He wasn't talking about prophets alone; He was talking to every believer. Jesus Christ meant that you and I may not be ordained by God to be prophets (as God gave every man different spiritual gifts), but we can still operate in the prophetic to the degree to which the Holy Spirit reveals to us per time. Isn't this awesome? That every child of God has access to the things of God through the help of the Holy Spirit?

So how do we operate and grow in the prophetic?

A Lifestyle of praise and worship

David became a prophetic king because he was a psalmist. And through the ministry of a psalmist, he received psalms from God that contain a lot of prophetic utterances. A life of praise and worship always leads to prophetic utterance. When the church in Acts 13:2 ministered to the Lord, the Holy Spirit said, "Bring me Paul and Barnabas". When people minister to the Lord, they place themselves in a position to receive from the Lord. Live a life of praise and worship.

In chapter 4, I shared how to access the prophetic and one of the ways was to accept the need for a prophetic covering which we saw in 2 Kings 3. Accepting the need for a prophetic covering was how kings Jehoram and Jehoshaphat and their army gained access to the life-changing power of prophecy through the ministry of Prophet Elisha. We can also learn from Elisha how he gained access into the realm of the prophetic. I believe there is something we always have to do to operate in the supernatural. Now let's go back to that same passage and see what Elisha did.

> "So the king of Israel went with the king of Judah and the king of Edom, and they marched on that roundabout route seven days; and there was no water for the army, nor for the animals that followed them. And the king of Israel said, "Alas! For the Lord has called these three kings together to deliver them into the hand of Moab."
>
> But Jehoshaphat said, "Is there no prophet of the Lord here that we may inquire of the Lord by him?" So one of the servants of the king of Israel answered and said, "Elisha the son of Shaphat is here, who poured water on the hands of Elijah." And Jehoshaphat said, "The word of the Lord is with him." So the king of Israel and Jehoshaphat and the king of Edom went down to him. Then Elisha said to the king of Israel, "What have I to do with you? Go to the prophets of your father and the prophets of your mother." But the king of Israel said to him, "No, for the Lord has called these three kings together to deliver them into the hand of Moab."
>
> And Elisha said, "As the Lord of hosts lives, before whom I stand, surely were it not that I regard the presence of Jehoshaphat king of Judah, I would not look at you, nor see you. But now bring me a musician." Then it happened, when

the musician played, that the hand of the Lord came upon him. And he said, "Thus says the Lord: 'Make this valley full of ditches.' For thus says the Lord: 'You shall not see wind, nor shall you see rain; yet that valley shall be filled with water, so that you, your cattle, and your animals may drink.'

And this is a simple matter in the sight of the Lord; He will also deliver the Moabites into your hand. Also you shall attack every fortified city and every choice city, and shall cut down every good tree, and stop up every spring of water, and ruin every good piece of land with stones." Now it happened in the morning, when the grain offering was offered, that suddenly water came by way of Edom, and the land was filled with water."

(2 Kings 3:9-20)

As we see from the above scriptures, Elisha was a man of committed praise and worship lifestyle. He said to the kings and the men with them to bring him a musician, someone to lead him in praising God and the Bible says the hand of the Lord came upon Elisha, and he began to prophesy. Praise and worship moves God as the Bible says "God is enthroned in the praises of His people" (Psalm 22:3). John also said in his letters that God seeks those who will worship Him in truth and in spirit (John 4:24). When we spend quality time before God in worship and praise, we will be able to move and flow in the prophetic more often. Without a consistent lifestyle of worship, it will be difficult for us to operate in the prophetic.

A life of prayer and fasting

Secondly, live a life of prayer and fasting. I have come to understand in my years of walking with the Lord that a man of much prayer and fasting will walk in an unlimited flow of the prophetic. In studying the life of Charles Finney, I discovered that the secret to his outstanding success was much prayer, which resulted in an unusual dimension of revelation. One of the key failures in the body of Christ is that when we don't understand a passage of Scripture, we run to man to interpret it for us. But we fail to bring that scripture to God and ask Him to reveal it to us. Sometimes we run from one commentary to the other and never run to the Lord who wrote it. There will be many things in the Word that we don't fully understand because we have fractional understanding but each time you come across one, you could bring it to the Lord in prayer and fasting. For example, take the life of Daniel. When he received something he did not understand, he always fasted and prayed for an understanding.

"Now while I was speaking, praying, and confessing my sin and the sin of my people Israel,
and presenting my supplication before the LORD
my God for the holy mountain of my God, yes,
while I was speaking in prayer, the man Gabriel,
whom I had seen in the vision at the beginning,
being caused to fly swiftly, reached me about the
time of the evening offering. And he informed
me, and talked with me, and said, "O Daniel, I
have now come forth to give you skill to
understand. At the beginning of your
supplications the command went out, and I have
come to tell you, for you are greatly beloved;
therefore consider the matter, and understand
the vision: " Seventy weeks are determined for
your people and for your holy city, To finish the
transgression, To make an end of sins, To make
reconciliation for iniquity, To bring in everlasting
righteousness, To seal up vision and prophecy,
And to anoint the Most Holy. " Know therefore
and understand, That from the going forth of the
command To restore and build Jerusalem until
Messiah the Prince, There shall be seven weeks
and sixty-two weeks; The street shall be built
again, and the wall, Even in troublesome times.
"And after the sixty-two weeks Messiah shall be
cut off, but not for Himself; and the people of
the prince who is to come shall destroy the city
and the sanctuary. The end of it shall be with a
flood, and till the end of the war desolations are

determined. Then he shall confirm a covenant with many for one week; but in the middle of the week He shall bring an end to sacrifice and offering. And on the wing of abominations shall be one who makes desolate, even until the consummation, which is determined, is poured out on the desolate."

(Daniel 9:20-27)

Daniel could walk in this dimension of the prophetic because he was a man of prayer and fasting. In verse 3 Daniel set his face towards the Lord to make request by prayer and supplications, with fasting, sackcloth and ashes. Prayer and fasting were the top secrets of Daniel in operating in the prophetic. Prayer is a powerful means of tapping into the mind of God concerning any given situation. It helps one to connect to God's future plans.

In Isaiah 45:11, God's word says:

"Thus says the LORD, The Holy One of Israel, and his Maker: "Ask Me of things to come concerning My sons; And concerning the work of My hands, you command Me."

(Isaiah 45:11)

Asking is prayer and praying is what connects you to the well of revelation in God. Whatever could be revealed would be revealed to us when we spend time with God in fasting and praying.

If you understand and walk in these four laws (Praise, Worship, Prayer and Fasting) that govern operating and growing in the prophetic, you will be protected from a lot of abuse. It is an important area to get into and when you begin to receive utterances from God, prophesy over yourself, write down what you can because it will surely come to pass. Be open to a person with the genuine gift of prophecy and let God's plan for your future be unlocked.

7

Grace to fulfil Prophecy

In conclusion, allow me to share something very personal with you - the power of grace in fulfilling the prophecy over your life. I discovered in God's word through the help of the Holy Spirit that one of the most powerful and important prophecies ever to come to pass in the kingdom of God happened by grace.

Ephesians 2:8, says *"For by grace you have been saved through faith, and that not of yourselves; it is the gift of God."*

The salvation of the world was the most powerful and important prophecy that was ever given by several prophets in the Bible. The prophecy of redemption supersedes every prophecy given from age to age. It has been fulfilled, it is still being fulfilled and it will continue as long as Christ tarries. The word 'by' in the above scripture means with the aid of grace, redemption was made possible. It is important that we recognize the grace of God in the pursuit of our destiny.

As I have mentioned earlier, to realize the promises of God for our lives, we need to take certain responsible steps otherwise they may never be realised. Now, your race in the prophetic will be fulfilled easier and quicker if it is run by God's grace. In 2006, when more fragments of the vision of our ministry, Grace House Int'l Ministry, began to unfold in me, God said to me that many are struggling all over the world. They are struggling because no man will by certificate, qualification or recommendation fulfil His predestined plan for their lives except God's grace is present in their pursuit of success. There is less stress on a bolt joint when it is well greased. Likewise, you will not need much strength when you are well graced by God.

Grace makes your journey easier. What took others one year will, by grace, take you six months. I have always said that apart from diligence, the speed and increase I am enjoying today in my life, family, ministry and business is purely the grace of God.

I understand and appreciate grace through the acronym G.R.A.C.E, which stands for **G**ift of God, **R**eceived from **A**bove to **C**reate **E**xploits. Without the grace of God, no one can fulfil prophecy. Apostle Paul, through the prophetic ministry of Ananias received a prophecy that God had chosen him to bear His name before the Gentiles.

> "Now there was a certain disciple at Damascus named Ananias; and to him the Lord said in a vision, "Ananias." And he said, "Here I am, Lord." So the Lord said to him, "Arise and go to the street called Straight, and inquire at the house of Judas for one called Saul of Tarsus, for behold, he is praying. And in a vision he has seen

a man named Ananias coming in and putting his
hand on him, so that he might receive his sight."
Then Ananias answered, "Lord, I have heard
from many about this man, how much harm he
has done to Your saints in Jerusalem. And here
he has authority from the chief priests to bind all
who call on Your name." But the Lord said to
him, "Go, for he is a chosen vessel of Mine to
bear My name before Gentiles, kings, and the
children of Israel."

(Acts 9:10-15)

In 2 Corinthians 15:10, Paul shows us how he was able to walk in the reality of this prophetic word concerning his future. He said,

"But by the grace of God I am what I am, and His
grace toward me was not in vain; but I labored
more abundantly than they all, yet not I, but the
grace of God which was with me."

(2 Corinthians 15:10)

Apostle Paul, who lived a life of the principles I shared in the previous chapters of this book, still acknowledged that the fulfilment of the prophecy over his life could not have happened by the principles alone but by the involvement of the grace of God. Many believers think the grace of God excuses them from certain covenant principles, like those shared in this book. Grace does not excuse us. What it does is to make what we have relevant in fulfilling our prophecy.

That is why for grace to find expression in your life, it will first of all incapacitate your capacity. In the book of Acts 9, we can see an example of this from God's word. God had to incapacitate Paul's existing capacity for His grace to find full expression in him.

> Then Saul, still breathing threats and murder against the disciples of the Lord, went to the high priest and asked letters from him to the synagogues of Damascus, so that if he found any who were of the Way, whether men or women, he might bring them bound to Jerusalem. As he journeyed he came near Damascus, and suddenly a light shone around him from heaven. Then he fell to the ground, and heard a voice saying to him, "Saul, Saul, why are you persecuting Me?" And he said, "Who are You, Lord?"
>
> Then the Lord said, "I am Jesus, whom you are persecuting. It is hard for you to kick against the goads." So he, trembling and astonished, said, "Lord, what do You want me to do?" Then the Lord said to him, "Arise and go into the city, and you will be told what you must do." And the men who journeyed with him stood speechless, hearing a voice but seeing no one. Then Saul arose from the ground, and when his eyes were opened he saw no one. But they led him by the hand and brought him into Damascus. And he was three days without sight, and neither ate nor drank.

Now there was a certain disciple at Damascus named Ananias; and to him the Lord said in a vision, "Ananias." And he said, "Here I am, Lord." So the Lord said to him, "Arise and go to the street called Straight, and inquire at the house of Judas for one called Saul of Tarsus, for behold, he is praying. And in a vision he has seen a man named Ananias coming in and putting his hand on him, so that he might receive his sight." Then Ananias answered, "Lord, I have heard from many about this man, how much harm he has done to Your saints in Jerusalem.

And here he has authority from the chief priests to bind all who call on Your name." But the Lord said to him, "Go, for he is a chosen vessel of Mine to bear My name before Gentiles, kings, and the children of Israel. For I will show him how many things he must suffer for My name's sake." And Ananias went his way and entered the house; and laying his hands on him he said, "Brother Saul, the Lord Jesus, who appeared to you on the road as you came, has sent me that you may receive your sight and be filled with the Holy Spirit." Immediately there fell from his eyes something like scales, and he received his sight at once; and he arose and was baptized."

(Acts 9:1-18)

The reason God does this is to give everybody an equal opportunity to fulfil their destiny without having to give an excuse of what they have or do not have. Verse 8 of Ephesians 2 says "not of yourselves; it is the gift of God". According to Paul, after you have done what you can do then the grace of God is what will make it happen for you. It is essential that we understand the power of God's grace in our lives, family, ministry and business in order to walk gloriously in it. Jesus Christ trained His disciples for three years to prepare them for their future responsibility of giving birth to the church of God.

> **"And with great power the apostles gave witness to the resurrection of the Lord Jesus. And great grace was upon them all."**
>
> **(Acts 4:33)**

Based on the above passage, the disciples did their part but the ultimate was the grace of God in the fulfilment of their predestined future as apostles. Our part in walking in and fulfilling prophecy is needed but God's grace is needed more.

My prayer is that as you submit yourself to, and apply the principles shared in this book, God's great grace will unlock your glorious future in Jesus' name. Amen!

Grace and Peace!

If you have been inspired by

UNLOCK YOUR FURTURE!

and want to contact the author, please write to:

femiadun.fa@gmail.com

For more copies / distribution enquiries,

please write to:

oeffiom@ghworshipcentre.com